LETTERS OF A MATCHMAKER

John B. Keane

Letters
of a
Matchmaker

THE MERCIER PRESS
CORK and DUBLIN

The Mercier Press Limited

4 Bridge Street, Cork
25 Lower Abbey Street, Dublin

© John B. Keane, 1975

First Published 1975

ISBN 0 85342 446 2

To

Mary Feehan

*Printed in the Republic of Ireland
by The Kerryman Ltd., Tralee*

INTRODUCTION

Poets, they say, are born not made. The same cannot be said of matchmakers. As will be seen from the following correspondence they are not created overnight. Only circumstances can make a matchmaker. In an ideal world there would be no need of such a person. Men and women would be paired off, the brave deserving the fair and, at the other extreme, every old shoe finding and old stocking.

There would be no surplus on either side, no left-overs, none left out in the cold. Rather there would be a man for every woman and a woman for every man. Alas and alack such an ideal climate is far beyond the hope or vision of mortal men. We must look, therefore, to our hero Richard Michael Richard O'Connor otherwise known as Dicky Mick Dicky to remedy insofar as it lies within his power this bleak and unhappy situation where men are often without women and women are often without men.

Dicky Mick Dicky O'Connor resides in that place known as Spiders' Well which is situated in the townland of Ballybarra which lies in turn in the midst of that wild and mountainous countryside along the borders of Cork and Kerry. Here he wrests a livelihood from five small fields and a haggard. The total extent of his holding amounts to fourteen acres. Two of the fields are meadows. They provide fodder for his five milch cows and pony across the lean seasons of winter and spring. The other fields are devoted to pasture and in the haggard the common vegetables and root crops which sustain man and beast are grown. The fields are wet and soggy for the greater part of the year but they are firm and fruitful in the long dry days of summer and autumn.

5

Dicky Mick Dicky is married to Kate McIntyre, a product of the misty westlands of the Dingle peninsula. She was ever a gay and cheerful woman who always took a firm hold of misfortune and fearlessly moulded it so that it enriched the lives of her husband and herself and strengthened their partnership. The pair are without issue having forfeited a young son to a raging plague of diphtheria and an even younger daughter to the diabolical blight of consumption.

Seven years have passed since they trudged arm in arm, wan and disconsolate, from the small mound in the Ballybarra graveyard under which lay buried the frail body of the little girl they had both loved. There she had joined her brother in eternal rest. There are many who would have succumbed to the grief and despair that arise from these lamentable, personal tragedies but Dicky Mick Dicky and Kate were moulded from finer clay. Other couples might have surrendered to the combined forces of scraggy soil, pitiless and uncertain weather, pestilence and death but it is fair to relate that the indomitable pair thrived rather than pined in this unlikely climate.

Dicky Mick Dicky's induction into the delicate business of matchmaking was caused by a number of factors. Small farmers of his ilk who peopled the hills and mountains around him were fast fading from the scene. There were no young folk left to take their places. The government was at pains to equal the opposition's record in afforestation and all available holdings were purchased with this in view. There would be trees in plenty but no people. There would be birdsong by day and at night the mooning vixen would call to the dog fox. The wind would howl and moan and carry the scent of pines to far-off places. The rain would whisper to the matted grasses but there would be no laughter, no crying, no playful shouting, no human sound at all.

Dicky Mick Dicky was determined that the people should stay in the hills and mountains. Life was brighter, better and longer. Men would come to see this in time. Soon unless something drastic was done a way of life would vanish forever. At this juncture we find Dicky Mick Dicky writing to his brother Jack who is a saloon-keeper, sole owner of the Shamrock Inn, Shillelagh Ave, Philadelphia. Dicky Mick Dicky has other brothers and sisters scattered all over England and the United States of America but of all these only Jack has kept in touch. The truth is that he needs the news and the feel of his distant source to make living more palateable. Like millions of his race he has never fully pulled up his roots nor has he been able to.

*　　*　　*　　*　　*

Spiders' Well,
Ballybarra.

My dear Jack,

I hope the weather over there is not like what we're getting here. We're all but drowned and what harm but I have five acres of hay down these nine days and the Pattern of Ballybunion staring me in the face. If the weather don't come fine soon it won't come fine at all and if it don't come fine at all my cows and pony will walk the Long Acre trying to nose out their pick across the coming winter. Since I wrote to you last I've turned my hand to matchmaking. There is a fostook of a man by the name of Cud Muldoon living alone in the holding next to ours. You will remember the mother and father Cornelius and Maynan Muldoon. Cud is bordering on fifty and he has Kate addled these past years buying socks and shirts and the odd suit of clothes for him. Too shy to go into a shop, a man with no woman, like many another around this place. The disease of the single life is a curse beyond curing when it catches hold.

Now over in Glenamoon there is a well-blossomed damsel living alone with her brother and she going by the name of Circes Fee. The brother Tom is anxious to bring in a woman but Circes has no notion of taking to the high road and she facing for forty. Word went abroad that she would not turn her back on a likely man with a roof over his head and the

7

means of supporting a wife. I got to work and soon, barring an accident, Cud Muldoon won't be turning and twisting in his bed as much as he used to. There was any amount of delving and digging to be done beforehand. Cud was never married before because he never set foot outside of Ballybarra in all his born days saving a trip to Cork for the Munster Football Final and he hardly married in the space of one July evening, not with a dial like Cud's with every tooth in his head as black as the ace of spades and the hair on his head standing up like the bristles on a coarse brush.

With Circes Fee 'twas different. She gave a tamaill in England but for sure she never married there. What took her there is another matter. Some say 'twas to leave a legacy to the Sisters of The Little Ones Lost. As the man said it do coincide. That was ten years ago. She left here eight months after the night of the Greyhound Coursing of Ballybarra and came back three months later much in the better of her visit with her natural shape restored and the pasty look gone from her face. So small blame to the friends and neighbours if they said she left a legacy behind her.

A man should always be careful of marriageable birds a certain distance of time after events like the Ballybunion Pattern, Ballybarra Coursing night and Listowel Races where you have all-night dancing, carousing and all makes of carry-on that priests and missioners does be always giving out about. There does be any amount of anxious dames with all their possessions intact, if you follow, what thinks they have carried their burden long enough and who does be well-tilled and seeded in those times and occasions I draw down. 'Tis after these outings you would find women softening in their attitudes to men they would cock their noses at before. There does not be many like these but there's enough to make a man wary. There's others then what often parted with it for a few pence worth of Geary's currant tops, what would think as little of giving of it as they would a mug of tay or a jug of colourin'. It all depends on the value you place in a thing and demand, of course, do have something to do with it too.

When word got out that I was tending to the wants of Circes Fee of Glenamoon who suits Cud Muldoon fine by the way, legacy or no legacy, didn't I get a letter from a lady anchored in a place called Coomasahara to the east of Caherciveen. She's tagged with the name of Fionnuala Crust, an only daughter burning oil I'd say but with a fortune of five hundred pounds. A man was what she wanted and she aisy about age as long as he had a house and a way of living and the natural faculties in fair working order if you follow me. I got on to Mickeen Snoss of Doonaleama who has a good place with seven cows and if he's long in the tooth itself he's still a fine lump of a man and some says what knows that he has a haft like the shaft of a dunkey's car. Once a good man they say always a good man. I arranged a meeting for Teddy O'Connor's public house in Killarney. We had a drink, small ones for myself and Mickeen Snoss and a port wine for Fionnuala Crust of Coomasahara. I left them at it and went down town to make out a dozen buns for Kate. They're to meet again and who knows but we'll have new blood in Ballybarra in no time at all. You'll hear from me no more now till the fall of the year and say a prayer let you that we'll get the weather fine or my cows and pony will go without hay.

Your dear brother,
Richard.

Coolkera,
Coomasahara.

Dear Mr O'Connor,

I have a lonesome tale to tell after landing you my fat fee, twenty pounds that left a nice hole in my purse. I'm back at home again after a month married to Mr Mickeen Snoss of Doonaleama. If I was teasing and tearing him till doomsday he wouldn't come to life. What mi-ah was on top of me to quit my fine home here. 'Tis cursed I was to travel the seventy long miles from here to Doonaleama with five hundred pounds of a fortune in my bosom and the same Mickeen Snoss not having a tack of the dick. What harm but I was looking forward many the lonesome year to having a man of my own and what do I wind up with only a lifeless latchiko with as much spark in him as a taovode of spairt.

I wanted him to go to a doctor to see after his apparatus but he told me he't let no man living look at it till they were washing him for the clay. So you see I would be well entitled to a refund of my twenty pounds. You contracted to supply me with a partner who would be well-geared to fulfil his part of the bargain. As I recall you boasted that he was a fine example of manhood. Well he fell down on the job entirely so I will thank you now good sir for my twenty pounds and I may tell you that you'll spare yourself time and money and maybe the back of Shaws to boot if I hear from you by return of post.

> Yours faithfully,
> Fionnuala Crust (Miss).

> Shamrock Inn,
> Shillelagh Avenue,
> Philadelphia.

Dear Dicky,

Got your letter. Tough shite about that chick from Coomasahara. You want to cover yourself from dames like that. Here in Philly we got what they call marriage parlours where a dame's got hundreds of guys to choose from. They got files and computers and they got head-shrinkers who conduct what they call compatability tests. You get a feedback from a computer says a guy aint suitable for a certain dame and that's the end of it. It saves a helluva lot of time and nobody gets hurt. Say you gotta guy aint got all his marbles or say a dumb guy who's a flop with the fancy talk and say this guy wants hisself a permanent piece of ass what does he do? He kicks in maybe fifty bucks to the dame or guy that

10

runs the parlour. That's for openers. I think they call it pre-
liminary pairing. He waits awhile until they come up with a
number of dames that cotton to his kind of kicks and sorta
general lifestyle. He kicks in maybe another hundred bucks
and a meeting is arranged. They hit it off and get married or
they just don't in which case there's no beef and the guy is
introduced to another dame. The more dames the quicker
the guy runs outa dough. There's one of these parlours on
the next block. It's called the Cumangettum Love Parlour. I
had a long spiel with the guy who runs it and he told me
you're just plain nuts to be working the way you do. He
says you oughta get out a circular advising prospective clients about charges and get them to reveal as much as possi-
ble about themselves. When you got all this dope you start
figuring who suits who. The other way you're gonna have
floozies coming up with decent Johns and nice dolls paired
off with maybe hoods or nuts.

This guy realises you can't have no set-up like he's got
over here and that they aint heard tell of computers in
Ballybarra but he figures your business oughta double if
you take his advice. I hope the weather's improved over
there. Here in Philly we got ourselves a twenty carat Indian
summer that's expected to last all Fall. You take care now
and give my love to Kate. You tell her Marge and me's gonna come for that holiday real soon now.

> Your loving brother,
> Jack.

> Hunter Hall,
> Ballyninty,
> Co Limerick.

Sir,
  It has come to my attention through hearsay that you
operate some sort of marriage bureau. I am a single man. I
still hunt. I'm in perfect health although sixty-eight years of

age. I am in need of a wife. For some reasons the local girls round here or those of my own class won't accommodate me. I am quite well off. I confess I sowed some wild oats and was interested in nice boys for awhile but which of us isn't human sir.

I was married but she left me nearly twenty-seven years ago for a professional tennis player. I would like a lass of twenty or so with good points, good health, good teeth etc. Must be of sound stock. I require no dowry but if one is available I would not be averse to taking it.

With regard to your fee sir. I shall pay according to quality i.e. ten guineas deposit if you accept the commission and a proportionate extra amount if she comes up trumps in performance. There is no point in your trying to pawn a flawed piece of material over on me. I'm as good a judge of a filly as ever drew rein.

Yours cordially,
Claude Glynne-Hunter (Hon).

Spiders' Well,
Ballybarra.

Dear Miss Crust,

As you call yourself. Although by laws of God and man you are no other than Mrs Michael Snoss and no man barring alone the Holy Father has the power to unfetter you. With regards to your twenty pounds the bargain is made and it can't be broke no more than you can make yourself a miss again.

Before you go engaging the law and maybe pauperising yourself into the bargain wait till you hear this. As I was letting go a grain of water at the back of a public house in town a few days ago who should arrive with the same complaint but your beloved husband Michael Snoss esquire of Doonaleama or, as he is affectionately known to his late wife, Mickeen Snoss.

He promised me faithfully that if you came back to him he'd go to see a doctor. Well now what have you to say to this?

I look forward to your reply.

Courtesy and civility assured at all times.

Your obt servant,
Dicky Mick Dicky O'Connor

Coolkera,
Coomasahara.

Dear Mr O'Connor,

I won't give you a dose of the law this time. I'll bide my time and wait the outcome of Mickeen Snoss's visit to the doctor. I'm afraid that there is no cure for what ails Mickeen bar alone a transfer from some fellow who would be going in the priests or brothers and would have no use for it.

Yours faithfully,
Fionnuala Crust (Miss).

Spiders' Well,
Ballybarra.

Dear Mr Glynne-Hunter,

Your two names will do you no good in these stakes nor your Hon. but as little but all the same you have as much rights as the next man and I'll take note of your wants. I takes no deposits but if you end up with what you want on my doing I'll bill you well for my dues. No doubt there is some women in cities or towns would be well pleased with an Hon. or a Lord or the likes but what good is such a thing in the country? Will it hurry your milking? Will it save your hay? Will you be the better the rutter for it? No my man it don't make no difference here no more we'll say than one blade of grass is more honourable than another or one bush

13

better than the next no more than one grey goose is more honourable than another grey goose nor one crow more than another nor a cat. However, you seem well fixed in material ways and this is always an advantage. A lone man in his own house is a powerful attraction. Say if you had an old sister now or the mother was alive it would be held against you. I enclose a circular which I would like you to read and a form to fill in to the best of your ability leaving out nothing as the priest said to the fornicator. The luck is with you as I say over you having no woman in the house for I'll tell you true that if you were to build a house from here to Australia it wouldn't be big enough for two women. Where you have two women under the same roof the marriage is under fire from the start. Two can make a nest but three can make hell. So my fine honourable man I'll be spotting form for you. You're a horsey man. You must know that outsiders seldom comes up and you're a thirty-three to one shot if ever there was one but the bookies were caught before and in this old life anything can happen. Where there's life there's hope. The dick don't give the men of this world no rest. He's a monster what lurks in wait from the first shave to the last. He's the world's greatest disturber and I seen sane men turned into idiots and wise men into fools by him. There is no connection between him and love. He stands for one thing only and that's the flesh whether 'tis triggered off by the rustle of a skirt or the whisper of a dropping knickers, whether 'tis the cocking of a leg or the bulge of a breast. Love is a fine thing, a noble thing but the other is a crazy fiasco and yet the two goes hand in hand like beauty and the beast or Sodom and Goodmorrow. Love won't drive a man to drink. Only the lad we spoke about can do that. Love won't put a man in a mental home but the other thing will keep him there maybe a lifetime. Love will make a home but the bucko will break it. Man you would want to harness of iron and a reins of steel to guide him from his first outbreak of his final one. There is no trusting him, no taming him and them what think they have him subdued is in for the biggest land of all for there is no bull nor lion nor no shark nor no serpent nor anyone of

14

God's creatures one tenth as treacherous. I'll say no more to you now my honourable man but I'll be mindful of you and please God the thing we were talking about won't be troublesome for you any more.

Courtesy and civility assured at all times.

Your obt servant,
Dicky Mick Dicky O'Connor.

Dead Man's Lane,
Ballylittle.

Dear Mr O'Connor,

I am a widow aged forty and something with it with own cottage and nestegg but the nights does be lonesome and I does be afraid with times the way they are. I want to know would you be on the look-out for a man for me. He must be under sixty and over forty with means. I don't care about anything else as 'tis company I want in the nights. I met you and your missus a few times and seen you at the mixed mission in Ballybarra Parish Church. Was there the night Father Scalp made the attack on the backs of motorcars and what goes on. More bastards he said comes out of them than all Paris or New York. My children are reared and the nice rearing they turned out. All in London without so much as a card from anyone of the five of them in the past two years not even at Christmas. Two of them married Protestants and I don't know about the others are they living free or what. I'll be good to a man, am good cook and tidy. That's all for now.

Yours sincerely,
Lena Magee.

My dear Jack,

The weather picked up great since I wrote to you last. I have the hay in the shed and the spuds dug. The turf is ricked and we have no dread of winter. Kate is fine. She is preparing for the Christmas and is now as I write mixing the groodles for the plum pudding. She says yourself and Marge is always welcome. Don't drop no line or nothing just come. I took your advice about the circular. We must await results. You will remember Lena Magee. Of course you would that married oul' Jack Magee of Dead Man's Lane. Well Jack turned over on his belly this Christmas five years ago and gave up the ghost. Lena is on the market again. She gives her age as forty. That would be true of her oldest daughter who was born prematurely a week after the marriage going on forty years ago. She has a nice cottage I must say, with a fine selection of ware and cutlery stolen from pubs, restaurants and hotels all over Cork and Kerry. Your cup might be stamped by the Great Southern Railway and your fork by the Imperial Hotel or your knife saying 'twas belonging to the Chinese Restaurant in Cork City. More power to her. 'Tis one way of making a home and she never made any attempt to rub off the names of the original owners. She'll tell you she was admiring a saltceller one day in the Great Southern when the manager arrived and made her a present of it. The same with the pepper-casters, mugs, jugs and bowls. All presents from managers.

About the circular. I had a job making it out. Some of the spelling might be better. I'm no professor. Ask me to dehorn a bullock or castorate a bonham and I'll do it blindfold but the pen is for men with soft hands what minded their books when I was looking out the classroom window and thinking about the Woodbine butt in my trouser pocket that I'd be lighting once as I left the school. Still for a man what quit after the fifth book I makes a fair fist of driving a pencil. Read the circular and see what you think.

ANNOUNCEMENT

Take notice that I Dicky Mick Dicky O'Connor being of sound mind in this year of our Lord am willing and able to perform services for those in a single or widowed state to wit the making out of a marriage partner for those as require same of their free will and consent, regardless of colour, creed or class with respect to the constitution.

Please advise as to weight, age, height, colour of eyes and hair. If widow number of offspring with ages and sex. If illegitimate please state for record purposes only. If deprived of natural faculties please state to felicitate my job and speed selection of suitable partner. Way of living. State full details, wages etcetera. If short a leg or hand or two or afflicted physically please state. Dependants if any. Drink heavy, moderate or teetotaller? Also state if randy or sex-mad etcetera. Frank answers earnestly required to felicitate enquiries. Set out below is rate of charges.

Farmers: One pound on head of cattle. Two pounds for horse or bull. Half crown on head of sheep or pigs. No charge on goats, asses, dogs, fowl but ponies, mules and jennets a half note.

Civil Servants: Including guards, postmen, pensions officers etcetera, one pound in every hundred of yearly income.

Professional Men or Women: Fifty pounds

Buttermakers: Two and a half percent of annual income

Shopkeepers: According to turnover

Tradesmen: All sorts, flat rate twenty five pounds

Counterhands, Floorwalkers, Dressmakers, Clerks and Labouring men, etc.: By arrangement

Other Matchmakers: No charge

Widows: Half price

No reduction in above rates no matter what.

* * * * *

Well my brother what do you think of that? 'Tis easier
than having to be searching the countryside looking up
chimneys and behind doors for partners to suit the odd mis-
fortunes what calls on me these days since my name is gone
out as a matchmaker. 'Twill give me more time to study the
nature of my clients and come to better conclusions as the
saying goes. The thing that worries me is will they tell the
truth and they answering the enquiry. They're not in the
habit of telling the whole truth here at all like they do in
America. Them computers of yours would be set astray in
no time by some of the answers you'd get here to innocent
questions. Most of them wouldn't answer at all only with
another question. You ask a man you might meet at Ballybarra cattle fair where he came from and he'd ask you
where you came from yourself. Even the priests asking questions at the confirmation does have a job with the simplest
questions. A Doonaleama man was asked who made the
world by the parish priest of Ballybarra.

'Whoever 'twas', said the Doonaleama man, 'they made a
right balls of it.'

So you see my dear brother what I'm up against. Still
they're so anxious to get women that they'll hardly go
making fool of me on account of 'tis themselves they'll be
fooling in the finish. What I used to do up to this was to go
to Ballybarra Bog during the springtime cutting or to the
football matches between the parishes. 'Tis there you'd often
see a likely man. Say you had the lone daughter of a farmer
with no brother for the place and she hankering for a sturdy
fellow to handle herself and the farm. Some of these would
go so far as to take a farmer's boy if all other fruit was failing and the same boy was a good physical specimen but

mostly 'tis for farmers' sons with no place of their own they'd be looking. 'Tis looks and size that matters here and money of course having a big say too. You may say there is no courtship and no romance but the marriages work well and that's what matters. They work better than most of the town and city marriages where its all cronawning, smahawning and pawdawling beforehand and none after. What I am you might say is the worm that curdles the loam of love.

We'll have the Christmas down on the door before we know it thanks be to God. Love from Kate and self.

Your dear brother,
Richard.

Coolkera,
Coomasahara.

Dear Mr O'Connor,

I tried your recipe and went back to Mickeen Snoss. He was with the doctor and he was told there was no cure for his ailment and 'tis me that knows it for didn't I give the past three weeks under the one quilt with him. I'd be better engaged sleeping with a corpse. Now like a good man will you forward my money by return of post.

Fionnuala Crust (Miss).

Spiders' Well,
Ballybarra.

Dear Mrs Snoss,

Am I supposed to go around like a vetinary surgeon examining and inspecting candidates or like a department man passing bulls. Did you try poitcheen on him internal and external? You're not doing your job right. Isn't it well known that doctors have no cure for what ails Mickeen. If they had they'd be millionaires. You'd be better off going to a nurse or a chemist's shop.

There is pills. There is bottles and lotions. There is blisters and whatnot there for taking that would improve his condition. Where there's life there's hope. There's roundy yokes called oysters what is swallowed alive out of their shells and what fills men with taspy what was only fit for the grave before. The poitcheen is your handiest remedy of all. I remember Nell Tobin's turkey cock Patsy what she used to stand on market days at the back of Emery's pub. After servicing three hens in a row the cock would be inclined to fall back and stagger and there would come a glassy look into his eyes. From under her shawl Nell would bring a black bottle. Inside would be a half-pint of poitcheen. She'd throw the cock on the flat of his back and pour a crawful down his piobawn. She'd follow this with a pill and in five minutes the cock would be anxious for more hens. If turkey cocks can be got going with pills and poitcheen why not old men?

Lamp oil or petrol rubbed into the backbone is another good way and there is them what swears by a turpentine blister applied to the afflicted area. Another way is coaxiorum. There is nine different ways of using this but two is all I know. One is to prick holes in an orange and put it between your breasts for two days and then give it to him to eat. By all accounts there will be no ram or no boar or no puck the bate of him after this. Another way is to fire a grain of your water on the back of his poll and he asleep. There is reported to be seven other ways and if there is any old woman handy she may know a few. Don't write to me no more letters now like a good woman but go back to your lawfully wedded husband and apply yourself to the job you were armed for.

Civility and courtesy assured at all times.

Your obt servant,
Dicky Mick Dicky O'Connor

Hunter Hall,
Ballyninty,
Co Limerick.

Sir,

Many thanks for your letter. I note what you say about the difficulty of procuring young wives these days. Perhaps I was a bit too choosy. You may now widen the net in the hope of attracting marriageable dames from the age of thirty-five downwards. This should not be too difficult. I am well endowed in every way. Meanwhile would you know of any nice boy who would like a good home. The work would be light and I promise to be very fond of him. Any sweet boy under forty would suit nicely.

I will be spending Christmas with my married sister in England but will be back for the New Year when I hope you will have some cheering news for me.

Yours cordially,
Claude Glynne-Hunter.

Spiders' Well,
Ballybarra.

Dear Lena Magee,

I am in receipt of yours and I would ask you to pardon the delay in answering but the truth of the matter is that I was casting about looking to know would I find a man what would be suitable for you. There is an honourable chap I have in my books that will be inclined to settle for a lady in your age bracket shortly but he must be given time. We wouldn't want him to think we were forcing the pace. That's a sure way to spoil your chances. This man I have in mind is a very well-bred sort of fellow and I'm sure you're a lady what has a lot of taste. All belonging to him were lords and squires and gentleman jockeys. He is a man of ideology, psychology, archaeology and bollixology and a great man too to fix a crack on a ceiling. He bulls his own cows as well.

You might say what the poet said long ago that he's a man for all sessions. I hear you have a lovely home with antiques and other valuables that you were presented with over the years. They say you are a woman of great taste and you tell me your age is a bit with the forty. What size of a bit if you please as my client will be anxious to know all these matters. Most men like him with farms of his size would be enquiring after laying hens such as district nurses, school-mistresses, hairdressers, lady doctors and the likes so we must consider ourself lucky indeed. I will be in touch in the very near future.

Assuring you of our continued attention.

> I remain,
> Courtesy and civility assured at all times,
> Your obt servant,
> Dicky Mick Dicky O'Connor.

> Shamrock Inn,
> Shillelagh Avenue,
> Philadelphia.

Dear Dicky,

First Marge and me sends our love to you and Kate. Business is good right now but the number of muggings in this so-called City of Brotherly Love is on the up every day. I enclose a few bucks. Let it go as far as it will as the guy with the small penis said the night he got married. That circular of yours sure oughta work wonders. I was assin around Fairmont Park in Philly last week and I got to thinking. Suppose you and Kate was to come out here for a holiday. Boy you sure would pick up a lotta knowhow in the Cumangettum. The guy owns it is going to be a millionaire. Two more years and he can tell the world to kiss his ass. What about it? You could stay with us. We'd love to have you. You'd meet all the guys from home. Man they sure would like to see you and hear the news. Don't worry about the dough. I can fix that. I got a pile stashed and I got buddies from home would throw you a benefit. You let me know man. You never gimme no news about the old place since you started on this matchmaking jazz. What gives? Who died and who buried 'em? Man I get crazy for news of home. I gotta go now. Joint's filling up. You tell Kate take care and how me and Marge would love to have the two of you.

Your loving brother,
Jack.

Menafreghane,
Tullylore,
Co Cork.

Dear Mr O'Connor,
    I am what people call a cripple. All that's wrong with me is that I have a wasted leg and a bit of a permanent stoop. I swear to you I haven't spoken to ten women in my lifetime. I am no good to converse with them and I am not a success at dances as you can well imagine on account of my disabilities. I am a small farmer and I live alone here in the high country in the townland of Menafreghane which is the Gaelic name for the Hill of the Fraochan berries which blacken the bushes here in the late summer. You know my trouble. I need a wife and have almost despaired of ever getting one. In my time I have been ridiculed by a few women I fancied. I have been pitied by others but alas I have been loved by none. I am aged forty-one and you are the last straw as far as I am concerned. I have a nice little farm, a good house but very little money as I had to give a fortune to a sister of mine when she married a year ago. I have my own bog, black as coal after the third sod and my piece of land is fertile. My creamery book would be a good witness for me if my appearance itself would be a hostile one. I like books and magazines and I have a keen interest in gardening.
    In God's name Mr O'Connor can you do anything for me? I am all but driven out of my mind with the need for a wife.

23

I often considered abandoning my way of life to commit myself to the mental home and other times I all but done myself in. All I want is a decent woman around my own age or a little bit older. I am not worried whether she has money or not. I am not worried about looks. What I want is a good woman, let her be plain as the gable of a house so long as she wouldn't laugh at me or pity me. Please show this letter to no one and I beg of you to do what you can for me.

Yours in hope,
Cornelius J. McCarthy.

Spiders' Well,
Ballybarra.

Dear Jack,

Spring came yesterday but you wouldn't know it for all the change it made. 'Tis wild and wet still after the winter. We had a good Christmas and I drank them dollars of yours on Christmas Eve. Kate had a jorum too.

I'll start with the news. Cud Muldoon that I matched with Circes Fee sired a second time, a daughter hot on the heels of a foxy-haired son. There is a servant boy working there and there is talk over he having a red head too. But do it really matter in the long run I ask you who took the shot once the flag is raised and the goal is allowed. You remember the damsel from Coomasahara what I matched with Mickeen Snoss. Well she's after leaving him again for the third time. She do maintain that he has no spark of life at all. She gave him a big dose of poitcheen on Saint Stephen's Day and it flattened him altogether. The hair turned white on him and what little of it he had but no other result and we all living in great hopes. I have made a few more matches since I wrote last but there is some poor wretches in the hills and there is no match on the face of this earth for their likes. The hills are rightly empty now boy. The rabbits and hares would hardly get out of your way there and the crows and magpies stand in the roads with no gorsoon to pelt a stone at them.

We were going great here till the Economic War when the unfortunate farmers had to pay the price for De Valera's notions. I remember a daughter of Nell Quade's by the name of Noney took off for England and came back in the space of six months covered with powder and lipstick with a new coat and hat and shoes and a handbag the size of a horse's collar and two big suitcases full of face lotions and slips and knickers and other finery. She drove the poor neighbours out of their minds with envy and the bitch had a highfaluting accent like poor Parson Roberts God be gracious to him the same as He would to a priest. When Noney was going back she took the daughter of a neighbour with her, a handsome girl of twenty by the name of Madge Heighery. The bother about England was that you needed little or no money to cross over and there was great houses there mad for cheap servants would pay the fare. 'Twas different with America. You needed dough to cross the Atlantic and not dough alone but medical tests and intelligence tests and references and you had to satisfy the American Consul and you had to have connections over that would claim you. 'Twas England scoured all the young women out of here. The boys followed. What better could they do except to mope around the crossroads or sit by the hearth with long faces and they scratching theirselves and thinking all the time of the fine women that went over the sea.

Whenever a girl came home for a holiday whether she was flying her kite for coin or in honest service she was sure to be better dressed than the aingisheoirs at home with her purse full of money and high-heeled shoes. She was a walking advertisement for the other side of the Irish Sea. They followed her back in dribs and drabs, in ones and twos and threes and finally in scores till there was more from the parish of Ballybarra in the city of London than there was in Ballybarra itself. Mark me well my brother but they'll be glad to come back yet. When that time will come I can't say but as sure as cocks crow and dunkeys bray they'll face this

25

way again.

I have no blame to the girls that went. They hadn't powder nor decent dresses only hand-me-downs of passion-killers to their knees tied with giobals or hempen cord and knickers made by their mothers out of Sunrise flour bags with sex-starved fostooks of men breathing down their necks what knew as much about paying court as a stallion or a bull. Who in the name of God could blame them for leaving this black land as it was in those days. Times were tough and bellies were slack. There was no diversion because everything that had to do with women was a sin. Thinking about them was a sin. Courting them and kissing them was a sin and sweet adorable Jesus loving them was supposed to be the biggest sin of all. Ignorance was everywhere, smothering us like the mist falling down from the hills. We couldn't see our way with it only grope like blind men not knowing whether we were going the right way or the wrong way.

By God there was slavery at the start of the thirties in this poor countryside. If a girl was knocked up with the fattening sickness she had no place to turn. She was shamed and scorned and damned and they searched high and low and begged, borrowed and stole for her fare to America or England rather than show love and understanding and what chance had the daughters of the poor unless they were made of steel and good Christ Jack no woman or no man is made of steel. A girl going in service to a farmer would want her legs fettered because in the dark of the night and she exhauted after her long day there were hard hands would go groping for her in the dark of her room. Many the good, innocent, hard-working girl that was wronged. 'Twas the time of the shut mouth and the closed eye and the hardened heart. There was too big black clouds covering the pleasant face of this country. One of them was the Church and the other was the State. They made prisoners of our minds and bodies and 'twas that bleak for awhile we were afraid to take note of the beating of our own hearts.

I'm not saying we were teetotally without good priests or brave men. It was worse for them, the creatures, than for

26

us. It was no time and no place for softness or charity. All we could do was turn to Christ in the quiet and wonder was He the son of God or was He the monster what the missioners roared about what sent the weak-willed and the unlucky scurrying like rats down the dirty road to Hell, with no come back for all eternity, no mercy, nor no allowance made for the fire in a man's body or the thoughts in his mind.

There is a few priests around here what gives out about my matchmaking as though 'twas an evil thing. Well my brother 'tis better than buggery and that goes on here and 'tis better than acting alone and that goes on here. They say there is no love in it. Is there talk of no love when the royalty and the lords and ladies are paired off or the high business houses? Man dear I will never know why the poor people of Ireland stayed so quiet in those times. Maybe they had their fill of fighting.

I don't know why people sing about love. Love is a disease that only time can cure and love is given to few so what is the singing all about. It's not natural for a man to sing when he's hurt or wounded so we may take it that he's not right in the head when he's bitten by the love-bug. Otherwise the poor whore would be lamenting and not making songs.

I saw a girl once and I twelve years married to Kate what mothered my two dead children and as loyal and as generous as ever shared her life with a man, a woman what stands back in the shadow of her man and compliments him with everything she says and does, a woman you just can't lose with and yet I saw this girl and I making for a bus in Killarney and she struck me the way a bolt of lightning strikes a tree and I was paralysed. She came on the same bus and she sat next to me and if I was there yet I couldn't manufacture two sentences to say to her although she passed weatherly remarks from time to time. I saw her often after that. She was a music teacher and she taught for a while in the convent in Ballybarra. Often and she out by way of Spiders' Well she would stop and talk to Kate or myself if one of us was showing on the roadway or in the door. You could see by her open face that she was eager to learn about the countryside and the ways of the people. By God I would teach her a lesson or two for no charge. Ah but sure I shouldn't be talking like this. Anyway if that was love, this thing I had for her, all it ever brought me was pain and sorrow. The image of her is faded now but in the odd time her face with all that young eagerness taunts me. But you must put these things to one side for mental diversion only and proceed onwards like the Civil Guard, at a steady pace.

Have I news enough given to you now? Kate is good Neither of us is anxious to go to America. We're happy and contented here and what we loved is in the clay here where we'll finish up ourselves as sure as there's paps on a heifer. We're thankful to you all the same and we'll be forever mindful of your kindness.

Your loving brother,
Richard.

Coolkera,
Coomasahara.

Dear Tricky Dicky,

Ah you scoundrel for there is no other handle suited to you. I went back to him again. I'm like a yo-yo between the two places. I dosed him and blistered him left, right and centre till I nearly done away with him. I poulticed his posterior with nettles but you would swear 'twas a tickle for all the notice Mickeen Snoss took of it.

There is no way to cure him. The battery is ran down too far by him and if you were to charge it for a week not a gigs nor a miocs would you get out of it. What mortification was on top of me in a country famous for the tackling of its menfolk that I should land a glugger. You will be good enough to return my twenty pounds. I got the law after Mickeen for the return of my fortune and I have no doubt

there will be a cheque soon in the post. If the money don't
come I'll put the law for sure on you.

Yours faithfully,
Fionnuala Crust (Miss).

*   *   *   *   *

It was thus as stated that Dicky Mick Dicky O'Connor
turned to the trade of matchmaking. As the first few years
passed his fame grew so that he became known in distant
places. In Clare and Cork, Limerick and Kerry if a man were
to announce that he hailed from Ballybarra there was sure
to be someone listening who would say: 'Isn't that where the
matchmaker lives?' and in the breasts of others the hearts
would flutter with hope and they would secretly vow to put
a day aside for calling on the one man who could help solve
the greatest problem in their lives. During these years Dicky
Mick Dicky was not the only person involved in the marriage business. There were fathers and mothers, greedy and
unscrupulous who cajoled, encouraged and forced young
daughters to marry men twice and three times their age.
Needless to mention these old men were well-heeled financially and had outsize farms to boot. These parents were
well rewarded for the sacrifice they were supposed to be
making. The truth of the matter was that the young brides
were making the real sacrifices, sacrificing their splendid
young bodies to the wrinkled hands of elderly lechers. Parents would argue that there was no harm being done as a
healthy young woman would be too much of a handful for
an old man and that after a few short years he would suc-
cumb to the demands of youth leaving her free to choose a
fine young man from the many landless bucks who would
sell their souls not to mind their bodies for a farm of land.
In some cases this was true but in the majority it was far
from being the case and there were many young women
who ended up in mental institutions as a result. There were

others who duped their senile husbands and took lovers. These would be servant boys who worked in the same house but these deprived and frustrated women were not above setting tender traps for postmen, insurance agents, agricultural inspectors and any other likely prospect who would have legitimate access to the house. Those made-marriages rarely worked. Matchmaking was different. Dicky Mick Dicky was a man who knew his countryfolk. He knew instinctively when couples were not suited to each other. When this happened he terminated his contract with the parties involved and advised them to look elsewhere. His great problem was finding matches for the physically deficient, for the over-sensitive, for the excessively sheltered, in short for all those who did not wholly correspond with the average picture of mankind and who because of this are often wrongly regarded as misfits and sometimes referred to by ignorant critics of the rural scene as mountain weirdies. Dicky Mick Dicky saw no weirdness only the grim reality of finding suitable partners for the maimed and the deprived among God's created men. If there was an over-riding policy to be found in his approach it would be this: that every sane and well-disposed man was entitled to a woman of his own in accordance with the laws of God, man and nature and likewise every woman entitled to her man. This inherent philosophy was to be the force that guided him when he was saddled with too many hopeless cases and there seemed to be no prospect whatsoever of marriage for the more benighted of his clients. Dicky Mick Dicky never gave up and even where anticipations were dimmest he managed always to keep hope alive.

Frequently he would be asked to defend his position. In pubs and in the market places of nearby towns coarse men in search of butts for their crude jokes would attempt to pillory him. He took it all in his stride and when hardened old toughs asked him jocosely to find a woman for them he would put them in their places by asking: 'Is it how you can't handle the one you have?' or 'Is your own one getting tired of you?' Underneath the jokes there would be an element of truth and there were many of the jokers who secretly regretted not having gone after the services of a matchmaker in the first place so unhappy and unsatisfactory were the marriages they had rushed into themselves. Dicky Mick Dicky knew that there were some husbands who would cheerfully unload their wives if there were a legitimate way of doing so. They secretly suffered their entanglements for the sake of their children or not to give it to say to the neighbours or to relatives. Underneath the banter was a great yearning for the love of an understanding woman. Dicky could afford to laugh if he so chose at his public detractors but he chose silence or a harmless reply for he was not a cruel man and he knew, if any man knew, how some women became careless after a few years, how they let themselves go so that they are no longer capable of attracting or exciting a man. He knew that there were many marriages which were mockeries. The slightest of hints or clues were sufficient to fill him in on the whole sorry tale. A word or two, a look, an act unnoticed by most were for him, more than adequate. He saw beneath the acting and the bravado and the pretence but he kept his counsel. Where was the glory in deflating a man who had already given a hostage to fortune. There was one occasion when one of the jibers went too far and passed a derogatory remark about his wife Kate. At once he smashed the man to the ground and there was another time when a beefy cattleman became too truculent and seized him without provocation by the lapels of his overcoat. In a matter of minutes the fellow was sitting on his well-cushioned rump with a rapidly swelling jaw. Dicky was not easily ruffled nor was he prone to violence but he was never a man to be bullied or cowed.

As time passed whether they liked it or not most men began to take him seriously as he intended they should. He believed in what he was doing. He felt as a man does who has a true vocation and he knew that without his services or the services of somebody like him the rural scene would fall further into the decay to which emigration had consigned it. We find him now writing to Jack of the Shamrock Inn in Philadelphia. It would seem as if he wished to justify his vocation.

*   *   *   *   *

Spiders' Well,
Ballybarra.

My dear Jack,

I hope this finds you as it leaves me with enough to eat and drink, yourself and Marge in good working order and all other things going as well as they can for you. I have now put together nineteen couples and only two of them discontented. One is the Crust Lady from Coomasahara and the other is a Mackessy man from Tubberdarrig West whose woman will only canoodle with him once in a year, that time being Saint Brigid's Day as she says there is no luck under a roof where you have that kind of disgraceful conduct going on all the time. No fun for Mackessy but once a year is better than no time at all which is what he was used to for close on forty years. The Crust lady is at her own home these past months but she'll be coming to Mickeen for the final time when the moon is in the last quarter as she was told by some old man down in that part of the world that this was a great time for the love caper. To my eyes Mickeen Snoss seems to be failing. There is a stagger in his walk and 'tis not drink is the cause of it and there is a stare in his eye so that I'm thinking it will take more than a quarter moon to extend his lease. He always made a bad fist of women for want of understanding their nature and their ways. If you asked Mickeen what love was you'd only dumbfound him and yet he knew a kind of love, love for the land and for the produce of the land. These things he understood and felt. If you saw the gratification on his dial and he rubbing the rump of a fat bullock or note him and he feeling the quality of grazing or meadowing the way he'd stroke the blades of grass or fiddle around for clover with the tips of his fingers or best of all to watch him with a fist of yalla wheat ears and he twiddling the seeds or letting them pour through his fingers feeling every single grain to know was it ripening proper. There is men like that what has the love knots tied the wrong way with them. Through no great fault of his own Mickeen always went withershins with women. Yet he was a powerful man in his heyday. I done my best for him and for any man what ever came to me and my best for any woman.

So we have remaining a total of seventeen working marriages that has all the signs of happiness and contentment with a half dozen toddlers and babes bawling and calling from one end of the day to the other. There is no other sound what guarantees so much the future of this countryside. 'Tis music to me to hear the cry of a child. So there you are. Without releasing a single button I'm after fathering six children for you may well say that only for me the craturs would not be there at all. What is a house without a child? Happy I'll grant like my own is but too many houses like mine could kill a countryside and what is a countryside without children? If marriages won't make themselves then I say we must go out and make them. Sure I would hardly be married at all myself if it wasn't for a matchmaker.

My wife Kate came from the West to work for a farmer by the name of Morrissey in Knockmaol. They're still there the Morrisseys with twice the amount of land for the whores never spent a copper nor never gave to charity and they worked their servants half to death. Kate came there as a milkmaid, a handsome cut of a girl, full of life with all sorts of mischief and roguery dancing in her eyes. My mother was in the house with me at the time but she was ailing and you may say the engaging of a partner was the highest thought in my head. I was the last of my family, yourself and all the others being scattered like feohadawn to the four corners of the world.

Morrissey was a slave driver. A boy or girl needed no reference to get a job from him unless alone 'twas a certificate to say that ate nothing and worked hard. Farmers were always on the look-out for boys out of orphanages who weren't used to the world or for big stupid fellows what would be wanting in the head, fools what settled for praise instead of pay for overtime. Farmers had no time for poetic chaps or gay men or sports or handsome fellows but the worst of all was a man with brains. Brains was the worst reference a fellow ever had because he was liable to read the papers and entertain notions of equality with his master which was a sin according to the missioners and the ranchers and a fearful notion worthy of hell to go carrying around in their pagan heads.

I saw Kate first at a crossroads dance on Snapapple Night and she dancing with one of Morrissey's workmen, a black-haired dullamoo with hair-oil and a tie-pin. I was taken by her at once and I danced with her a few times but I put no spake in about what I had in mind. Instead I went to see Falsetooth Riordan of Ballinruddera who was a kind of matchmaker. He demanded a pound down and three more if she agreed to marry me. I had three pounds spared and not another copper to my name. I handed him the pound and a week later he told me that the girl had no notion of marrying, that herself and her parents were dead set against it and that she was sparing her service money to go to America. The next I heard was that Falsetooth was matchmaking on behalf of a strong farmer from Knockmaol itself by the name of Hognose Hogan and that he was given a five pound note down if he could inveigle Kate to settling in Knockmaol. I tried a new matchmaker by the name of Keating from the Stack Mountains, an honest class of a man who would take three pounds when and if I was latched to Kate. This was a silver-tongued loveable man with sentences that ran from one minute to ten and lovely long words like you'd hear in a poem. He took my account to Kate and he made a strong case for me. Meanwhile Falsetooth was working like a demon for Hognose but his man was well into the fifties if he was rich itself whereas I was only twenty three and a lively, likely make of a man. We went west in a jennet and trap on the first day of June taking Kate with us to the home of her parents. They spoke

34

bad English but their Irish was fast and free. Keating produced a bottle of whiskey and Kate's people produced glasses. Then Kate and her sisters took off for the shore while Keating made my case. He was the most marvellous liar I ever heard and while he talked about me I was so carried away that I thought I was listening to the life story of some saint. Then when he came to describing my few cows and bit of land you would swear that it was the Garden of Eden itself. The main thing on my side was, of course, that Kate was for me. The parents spoke about America but Keating said he gave seven years there as a potato-taster and that hell was a pleasanter spot. He was never beyond the town of Tralee till that very day but to listen to him you would swear he knew America like the back of his hand. He had a great run of talk for a man that was used only to bog and mountain. Bit by bit he won my woman for me and finally 'twas settled. The best they could offer in the line of a fortune was ten pounds but 'twasn't a fortune I wanted but Kate. We drank more whiskey and Kate's father and Keating started to talk about oul' times. Then I saw Keating's eyes narrowing as he looked out of the window along the white ribbon of road what went for miles in a long loop above the sea.

'Christ Almighty', he whispered to me, 'that's Falsetooth and Hognose. I'd know the gait of Hognose's cob if he was as far away again.'

We made our excuses and collected Kate. She hadn't much belongings save a silk shawl what her grandmother willed her and she has that same shawl to this day. She had a pillowslip full of clothes and an old sciath full of odds and ends the mother gave her. On the road we passed the pair inside in the cobtrap. Hognose was pouring sweat and so was his cob with white foam like suds all over him. Hognose Hogan had small black eyes like currants stuck in his pudding of a face. He knew he was done when he saw the three of us together. 'Tis certain that Kate's parents would never consent to myself if they knew the extent of Falsetooth's farmlands and his name for being rotten with money.

'I'll give you a hundred pounds', Hognose shouted to me, 'and the service of my bull 'till the day you die if you draw out of this and leave the girl to me.'

'Not', says I, 'if you give me a million and my cows', says I, 'are no fools and they in and out of the Long Acre since they were heifers. They know the gaps and they knows a bull when they sees one and a bull knows them.'

Hognose swore and he cursed and he spat but we were first off our mark. I married Kate the following December 'Twas a frosty time and I was caught short of money having to fork out five pounds to the parish priest and another pound to the parish clerk and to land up thirty shillings for a firkin of porter for them what would come sopping.

I went to the town of Listowel to a turf dealer a week before with a pony-load of heavy turf for 'twas by the weight they bought it. 'Twas so wet it froze the night before and I had to sell before the noon of the day so that the sun wouldn't come and melt it. It made four shillings for me. The following day I sold another rail to a schoolteacher before it thawed for four more shillings because 'twas my aim to hire a motor car for a visit to Limerick on the day of our honeymoon. We would go to the pictures what I longed to see since they came out and maybe have a mouthful of tea somewhere at an eating house before coming home. In Listowel I went into a public house for a bottle of stout. At the back there was a clothes line of clothes that had two white shirts drying on it. I took these and I'm sure I didn't leave the owner short. There was plenty others.

We had a great day in Limerick where neither of us never was before. In the pictures we sat on very high seats. We found out later that they were what are known as tip-ups. We never thought to lower them down as we didn't know anything about such seats and thought they were made that way on account of city people being smaller and having such narrow bottoms. We had ham and tea in an eating house followed by buns but the charge was saucy although we enjoyed it. We came home happy and nature took over then. The Lord have mercy on Keating that kindly Prince of men. He was a gay man and a great matchmaker. 'Twas the drink that killed him. Only for his handsome talk and his wiles and his roguery I would have been no match for Falsetooth and Hognose. In time Falsetooth made out a woman for Hognose, a bouncer with fat red legs, an almighty rump and fingers like sausages. But she done him fine and when he buried her he stood a grand cross over her grave. I'll leave you now and bless you. There is fine days coming soon according to Old Moore and there will be great times for all makes of people. Give our love to Marge.

Your loving brother,
Richard.

Spiders' Well,
Ballybarra.

Dear Widow Crust,
I got your letter and I will come to its contents later. First of all I must sympathise with you on the loss of your beloved husband, the late Mickeen Snoss. The Lord be good to him and grant him a silver bed in Heaven. He is at rest now have no doubt amongst the angels and saints for God knows the poor man suffered his share of purgatory in this world and no disrespect intended to yourself for you played your part nobly and in no way can you be faulted. God knows you acted above and beyond the call of duty and there is few women with the patience and perseverance shown by you in your misfortune and misery and when your own time comes to join Mickeen there will be a silver bed for you too in the halls of Heaven for although the horse that earns the oats don't always get them in this world he won't be left short in the next and there is many the waster resting on his oars in this vale of tears will have his rump well singed when he passes over to the other side. Now for the contents of your letter. You must remember that no daisy has appeared over Mickeen yet and it might

be too previous if you were to put yourself on the market right away although no one has a better right. I think you would be well advised to bide your time till the fall of the year or at least until the summer is down and the grass has a chance to show itself over your husband's last resting place.

I have in mind for you an uncommon man, a blacksmith and a small farmer with the strength of a horse and he barely gone the forty-five years with a curly head and all his own teeth and no fear of he failing with we-all-know-what for didn't he leave his curls on several and he sowing wild oats while he was working as a journeyman hither in Clare. Carrolane is his name from Coolnaleen and the reason he never married was because his name for calefacting bastards went far and wide and the parents of likely women were wary of him the poor fellow. I think he might be the man for you. Now no one knows better than me that there is a lot of luck in the making of matches but I assure you that lightning will not strike twice in the same place as far as you are concerned because I can assure you that this is one horse of a man in all departments.

So my advice then to you is calm yourself till the fall of the year and I'll go matchmaking for you. Please God you'll be Mrs Carrolane in due course and there is more good news for you. I only charge half the fee for widows.

Courtesy and civility assured at all times.

Your obt servant,
Dicky Mick Dicky O'Connor.

Menafreghane,
Tullylore,
Co Cork.

Dear Mr O'Connor,
I suppose you could find nobody for me. Remember me! I'm the man with the wasted leg and the stoop. I knew it

wouldn't be easy on account of my disability. I know how busy you must be so I'll just remind you again to be mindful of me should you come across any kind of decent girl for me. For God's sake do what you can for me as I can find no words to tell you about the loneliness.

Hoping to hear from you at your earliest convenience.

Yours in hope,
Cornelius J McCarthy.

Hunter Hall,
Ballyninty,
Co Limerick.

Sir,

I was hoping to hear from you but no doubt you are kept going. In your last letter you mentioned the difficulty in finding young wives for old fogies like me. You may recall I wrote and told you to widen the net and I suggested we try an enlarged area from the age of thirty-five downwards. Obviously you have had no luck. Since I live alone I have given much time and thought to my particular problem. Here I am sixty-eight years of age with most of my allotted span foolishly squandered and nothing whatsoever to show for my time. How vain of me to expect young women to come flocking to me at my time of life. My wrinkles grow more pronounced and the infant scholar would not be hard put to count the hairs on my head. Yet I am not altogether wasted. I am a sprightly fellow for my age and I could still be of service to a woman. It's dashed lonely here most of the time. I now suggest that you widen your net further. Say we extend the age to under forties or say you were to come across a well-preserved firm type of woman a little older be she widow or spinster I would be well pleased. I am fully aware of the fact that I am not getting any younger and that my chances grow slimmer every day. I would ask you, therefore, to expedite the bally business and make allowances for my impatience. Every day that passes is another black mark against me. There is another thing I would like to bring up. On each occasion on which I have written to you I have asked if you might be aware of the whereabouts of a nice boy under forty, preferably under twenty but again beggars cannot be choosers. I should imagine that there should be little difficulty here as the demand seems always to be for women. Consequently I am somewhat surprised that you have never mentioned the matter in any of your replies. Please give the matter your kind consideration and I shall not be unmindful (financially) should you succeed.

We are agreed then about the age extension in respect of my future wife. There will surely be somebody interested now that the post is open to all-comers as it were. I hope to hear from you soon.

Yours cordially,
Claude Glynne-Hunter.

Spiders' Well,
Ballybarra.

Dear Cornelius J McCarthy,

I have not forgotten you my honest boy and there is no day that passes that I don't think of you and your lonesome situation up there in them deserted hills. It is not easy to place you and we both know why so I won't go into that. I promise you this, however. You won't be forever without a woman. Rome wasn't built in a day. It is only a matter of time, a matter of persevering till we get what you want. I never takes note myself of ailments like you have. There is more to a man than hands and legs if people would only see. A good heart is everything and I know from your letters that you have that same heart. I would judge you too to be a man of mettle what would not be afraid to defend his corner. Don't despair. There may be nothing on the horizon now but in this game it's when you least expect it that the sun comes out. One day there might not be a single woman available in the entire countryside and the next you'd find yourself being knocked down by every sort of a long hair. Like all businesses there is ups and downs. Keep your fingers crossed. You may be small and thin as you say and you may have a bad leg and a stoop but you have your own place and you sound like a decent man so compose yourself and be content to wait. You may be sure and certain that your turn will come too when you least expect it.

Courtesy and civility assured at all times.

Your obt servant,
Dicky Mick Dicky O'Connor.

Knockbrack,
Tubberdarrig West.

Dear Dicky,

I am now well married and scalded thanks to you. This wife of mine must think she's a cow or something. She'll only leave the bull near her once a year. What am I to do? All my pleadings is in vain. I told the curate and I told the parish priest and they spoke to her and the answer she gave was that no one came to our Divine Mother Mary and she did fine regardless. I busted in then and said I was flesh and blood and the oul' parish priest told me conduct myself and not be making a bashte of myself and to know was there no other thing in the world except corpulation I think he called it and asked me why we weren't saying the Rosary at night and know when was I at confession last or did I know the value of Sanctifying Grace. I turned to the curate and he only shrugged his shoulders the poor fellow and I could see that if he put a spake in there would be trouble for him. I got no law from the parish priest save to conduct myself and be mindful of my wife's health and feelings and to thank God for the two fine healthy children I had and

not be like a stallion that was always inclined to rear up.
The curate came later on his own and he had a long talk
with the wife but no use. She locked the bedroom door and
I could hear her praying all night. 'Twas like a monastery
from that till cockcrow. 'Tis no joke being yoked as I am.
Yourself is a man I sets great store by. Maybe you'd know
of some way of coming around her. I have heard of Coaxiorum but you know as well as me there is no such a thing.
I'll be on the look-out for word from you. You're a man
that knows the ins and outs of delicate matters.

Yours faithfully,
Thady Thade Biddy Mackessy.

Spiders' Well,
Ballybarra.

Dear Mr Glynne-Hunter,
Yours to hand on Monday last but it being a day I had a
mehill of men engaged I postponed answering. I was took
up most of the week cutting my year's supply of turf which
I sells the week before Listowel Races so's I'll have a pound
or two to play with. My fine honourable man I have some
news for you. There is a handsome widow just gone the
forty that has a desire to meet a respectable, well-away man
with a view to matrimony. Her name is Mrs Lena Magee
from Dead Man's Lane in the village of Ballylittle. Her pre-
cise age I cannot tell you as ladies are not hasty to release
news of this nature but if appearances means anything she
can't have all that mileage up. She is a most intellectual
model of a female with a nice cottage and a fine collection
of crockery and silverware and other costly items that she
gathered one way or another from time to time. She is a
famous cook and without wanting to bellows her coals too
much I can guarantee that this is a lively bit of gear. You
would be well advised to entrust me with the arrangements
of a private meeting between the pair of you in some warm
snug of a public house in Ballylittle or elsewhere where no

one will be the wiser about the business in hand. Over a drink or two ye can be whispering and swopping soft talk. Ye can be humming and hinting and let there be a taste of a kiss and a bit of a hug thrown in if all goes well. A good honest house is Morgan Shaughnessy's of Dead Man's Lane in Ballylittle village where there is no spitting on the floor or roaring or stamping. I'll have her there bar a fall at four o'clock on Sunday evening next. You'll have no trouble in finding the village. 'Tis well signposted after Abbeyfeale. Dead Man's Lane is on the left off the main street as you come from the east.

There is another tricky matter which you drew down in your last letter and that is concerning a nice boy who you say you would give a good home to and treat very nicely and all to that. I don't go in for no dealings in boys as I think a man should have more respect for his water-spout. However, every man's business is his own and I won't go no further on this subject. If the arrangements as regards Sunday don't suit you please let me know by return of post. Bring a bag of toffees with you. She likes toffees.

Courtesy and civility assured at all times.

Your obt servant,
Dicky Mick Dicky O'Connor.

Spiders' Well,
Ballybarra.

My dear Thady Thade Biddy,
    Yours to hand. Holy God but you have a lot to endure. There can be no harder lot than yours. I know men would put the double barrel to her head if she was to cut off the supply. I never heard the bate of it in all my days and why Saint Brigid's Day of all the days of the year. I know next to nothing about Brigid bar alone that she's the Patron Saint but I'm sure saint or no saint, she wouldn't wish to support your wife's carry-on. You have two ways to dealing with this

matter and I'll tell them to you now. You can lock her out at night till she comes to her senses from the cold but this is a hard thing to do to a woman even if it is well going to her itself. Your other alternative is this. I'm sure the two of you does sit down for a mug of tea or cocoa before ye goes to bed at night. If this be the case you could start by doctoring the cocoa unknown to her. Better wait till some night she have a cold in the head when her sense of taste will be wanting and then when you get her back turned slip a small dollup of poitcheen or whiskey into the cocoa. After the first taste she won't notice when you lace the cocoa better. Bide your time—and let the drink do the rest. You may be sure she won't be the same woman after dosing her. There's many a man Thady with your trouble but God nor man won't make them admit it. There's many a woman too but 'tis the fashion for generations to stifle all natural sorts of love notions and what do this lead to. It leads to too much thinking and no threading and where you have that sort of unnatural mortification you have a collapse of the brain. Mind now what I told you. I'll be most anxious to hear what way you got on.

Courtesy and civility assured at all times.

Your obt servant,
Richard Michael O'Connor.

Spiders' Well,
Ballybarra.

Dear Fionnuala,

I feel I have known you long enough to call you by the first name. Our man Carrolane is anxious to vet you and 'tis my way of thinking that you'd be anxious for a gander at him. He's a fine, big, hairy man and there is surely a space of two feet between his chest nipples. He's the last of his breed and need I say that he'd like to put his stamp on a few gearrcachs of his own. He was borned an American citizen but the father and the mother came back to Ireland and

44

died young. All the father's folk were swept away by ship fever and gonorrhoea and the mother's by galloping consumption so 'twas a miracle that the poor chap turned into the grand block of a man he is now. The forge is doing well and he is a man that's highly respected by his neighbours. As you may know 'tis often the wont of small and middling-sized men to chance their arms against giants. They do this to make a name for themselves. One night after a wrendance he was provoked beyond endurance by a carload of craven cafflers from some distant town. The upshot was that he ran through the wretches like shite through a goose, leaving four stretched 'flat and two more holding their undercarriages like they'd be scalded. 'Tis many a long day now since Carrolane had any truck with women so you may say that he has catching up to do. He'll make for you the first night like a cow making for aftergrass. Hold steady for the present and compose yourself. There is good times coming soon. What would you say to a meeting in the snug of Ted O'Connor's pub in Killarney. 'Tis a cosy spot and many what went into it single came out doubled but I hope now in earnest that you won't be expecting too much from the man. Enough is enough. Be patient and kind and you'll get as good as you give. There is one thing about marriage that people should never forget and this is that one and one makes one and not two. Hoping to hear from you soon.

Courtesy and civility assured at all times.

Your obt servant,
Dicky Mick Dicky O'Connor.

Shamrock Inn,
Shillelagh Avenue,
Philadelphia.

Dear Dicky,
Guess what. The Cumangettum Love Parlour is closed and the guy that used to own it is doing one to ten in the state

pen. It was all a racket. He was doing alright in Philly but the Feds busted him when he opened a branch in Baltimore. The guy was a crook. The computers were phony. Him and his operators were phony. He had a ball while it lasted. He had a fat blonde broad used to work for him but she got away. No trace of her, holed up somewhere I guess waiting for him to be paroled. There's a helluva lotta dough stashed away somewhere maybe in safety deposit boxes or in the broad's name. Who knows. I liked the guy. Now I gotta favour to ask you. There's an ole guy belts it goodo here most nights name of Robert Emmet O'Bannion. The guy's mother was a narrowback. I guess his grandfather or grandmother musta been Irish cos he don't never let up yakkin about his mother and the Emerald Isle and Irish colleens and four leaved shamrocks and little bits o heaven and all that sorta crap. Man he's about the corniest, mushiest ole Yankee Irishman you ever did see. He's the original Irish Mick and then some but what matters is the ole guy's loaded. Some say he's a cousin to Dion O'Bannion but he don't never make no mention of Dion's name so who's to say. One thing is sure. He carries a rod and a black-jack and he knows how to use 'em. If he's gonna be rolled he aint gonna roll alone. I guess he's seventy if he's a day. Sometimes he calls a taxi and I seen cabmen hand him call-girl cards but he don't pay no heed. He's got his eyes set on an Irish colleen. He believes the only pure girls on the face of this here shit-pile is Irish colleens. Sometimes the guy cries when he talks about his mother and some colleen he knew when he was a kid. This colleen married a cop and he never saw her no more so now he wants a real Irish colleen and he says his gonna go back to the old country to get one. Maybe you can help him. You surely got some kinda colleen to suit the guy. He's old and his sight aint what it used to be and the way he drinks the colleen's sure gonna be a widow before the first wedding anniversary. Can you do something? He don't haggle when it comes to the pay off. I'll say that for the old guy. You see what you can do and I'll keep him on ice till you come up with something.

Marge is fine, just fine. You just wait. You're gonna see the two of us stepping out of a cab one day real soon. Write and gimme all the news when you get an hour to spare.

Your loving brother,
Jack.

Coolkera,
Coomasahara.

Dear Dicky,
The sooner the better. After the non-starter you fobbed over on me the last time I would be well entitled to the best you have. O'Connor's snug in Killarney would suit me fine. There is buses back and forth the whole time between Coomasahara and Killarney. Some of them bus drivers are fine able men, well-fleshed and solid. 'Tis my guess that they'd be lively at night over they being sitting down all day. This Carrolane you have for me sounds like a likely mark. I would be most anxious to leave no grass grow so fix the meeting for soon. I have only one life and the Catechism don't say nothing about courting or coupling in the hereafter. I don't want to die without the imprint of a man. Make the meeting for Sunday week or for the Sunday after at the latest.

Fionnuala Crust (Miss).

Knockbrack,
Tubberdarrig West.

Dear Dicky,
My great friend. May the buds quicken for you and the sap run. May all your sails be full of gales and all your fields be green as the poet said and as I say to you now and I looking out of the window into the face of a sickle moon. May the stars shine for you and the rivers sing for 'tis you that

47

has brought me from the black valley of despair to the mountains of delight. Your advice was sound. After getting your letter I bided my time and sure enough didn't she complain this night soon after of having a blocked nose and a cold in the head. Ha-ha says I to myself and ho-ho and hey-hey we'll put Dicky Mick Dicky's cure to the test. There she was in front of the fire and the head bent by her and she sniffing and sneezing like a badger rooting in a wood. I think I'll go to bed says she. Don't says I till you have your mug of cocoa. Oh I couldn't bear cocoa tonight says she my nose is that stuffed. Try a drop of hot milk says I with a pinch of white pepper in it. I'll chance it so says she although I know for sure 'twill do me no good. I got my muller and poured in my milk. I sprinkled it with white pepper and while the head was still bent by her I took out a noggin of poitcheen from my breast pocket and laced the milk with a likely dart of it. Down goes the muller to boil and up comes the bubbles in no time. Here says I and I filled a mug for her. She took it and drank a small tint, then another tint and then a good swallow. I owe unto God says she but the white pepper is great stuff entirely. I find my nose loosening and my head clearing already. Finish the drop you have left says I and I'll make more for you or better still says I go up to your bed and I'll put a bit more pepper in it. She was said by me. As I was working in the kitchen I could hear her talking away to herself and humming and giggling and she getting ready for bed. 'Twas what you might call a contented sound. I doubled the dose of poitcheen and swallowed what was left in the bottle myself as a precaution against germs. When the milk came to the boil I filled up her mug again and made for the bedroom with the hope soaring in my bosom. I held it under her mouth and gave her sup after sup and by the hokey didn't she drain every last drop of it. First she cried and then she sighed and then she laughed. I got in beside her and I hadn't my head on the pillow when she wrapped her two hands around my neck and her two legs around my back. We must get more pepper tomorrow says she. I won't tell you no more now except to say that no man be he black, white, brown or yellow ever spent a better night. I sold a yearling the day before yesterday at Bannabeen cattle-mart and invested in pepper. As you often says yourself there is good times coming. I'll be forever in your debt.

Your devoted friend,
Thady Thade Biddy Mackessy.

Spiders' Well,
Ballybarra.

Dear Jack,

Everything is fine at this side and going through my books the other night I counted forty marriages in the past seven years since I set up on my own. This client of yours what wants the Irish colleen. Would he be suffering from bullocks' notions? If he's seventy that's the time of life for them. Oul bucks of that age does be forever pinching ladies behinds and tickling them and generally squeezing them when they thinks no one is watching. 'Tis the final kick before they let go life for good and no great notice should be taken of them and full allowance made for their last capers. Still you say in your letter that he does not follow call-girls. What is call-girls? Is it women that would call you in the morning for work or that would be working for you and would call you if somebody wanted to see you like secretaries or clerks and what not? I know the kind of colleen he has in mind, a rosy-cheeked damsel, all smiles with long red hair and a rose in it and she sitting at a spinning wheel or knocking notes out of a harp in the sunshine outside a thatched cottage with the wallflowers everywhere and the mountains in the distance and the oul' mother sitting in the doorway with her hands folded and she showing off an almighty amount of red petticoat. You know as well as I do that there's no such creatures in this country no more than there is leprechauns or lorgadawns or banshees or Jack O' the Lanterns. He might get one in New York or Chicago but

49

there was never the likes of those colleens seen in this corner of the world barring at a fancy dress parade or a concert. Find out more about him if you can. You say he's well-heeled. Could you give me a rough idea of how much he has altogether? What age exactly he is not that this will be worth much because he'll hardly tell the truth anyway. I had to stop sending out them circulars over the pack of lies I was told. You'd get a one from a fellow saying he had blue eyes and that he was tall, dark and handsome whereas he might have a squint or be half blind and instead of being tall, dark and handsome he's be tall, grey and dirty. The same with the women, ones fifty pretending to be thirty and ones seventy pretending to be forty and there was one with a wooden leg what said nothing about it. The match was nearly made but 'twas the luck of God I ran across a shoe clerk in a public house that told me about the leg being wooden. I hired a hackney car that minute and went to the house where she lived. What do you mean says I not telling me you had a wooden leg? What's wrong with a wooden leg says she so long as the other thing isn't wooden? Nothing says I but you didn't tell my client or myself. You never asked says she. What would make us ask says I? You think I ask every woman I meet has she a wooden leg? Ah look here says she and she caught me by the hand. A wooden leg is like an adopted child. With all the ups and downs of life it could be better to you than one of your own in the end. Kate is in bed with a dose of the flu this past week but she expects to be up any day now. Give our regards to Marge and send the reverent information.

> Your dear brother,
> Richard.

> The Tailrace,
> Feale River Cross.

Dear Mr O'Connor,
    I am the Murphy girl from the Tailrace that got married

50

lately to Tom Cuddy of Been Hi . I am enclosing the money that's due to you. All our thanks are due to you too. We are very happy although 'tis only a month since the knot was tied. Life was so lonely for the two of us especially and we so backward and tuathallach not knowing how to put one word on top of another in the company of strangers. You changed all that and I am sure that there is a happy future before us. What a shy man and what a grand man and what a loving man is my husband. Politer you wouldn't meet in a dreaper's shop. The night we got married he was slow about getting down to business but once he started he gave a good account of himself. He's so mannerly. In the morning he gave me a little tap on the shoulder.'I beg your pardon Miss Murphy', says he, 'but could I trouble you once more.'

Gratefully yours,
Catherine Morley nee Murphy.

Coolkera,
Coomasahara.

Dear Liar and Gallows fodder,

May Jesus and His Holy Mother and Blessed Martin and all the saints and martyrs come to my aid although 'tis me that's the real martyr. The clock is after striking twelve and down from the room like the mumbling of thunder in the McGillicuddys comes the snoring and grunting of my lover boy. We went to bed at nine and put out the lights. We lay side by side not stirring nor moving like two gamecocks each waiting for the other to make the first move. The next thing I heard was a yawn and after that a snore that would lift the roof from a hayshed. I thought of your words so I composed myself. I waited and waited till I heard the clock striking ten. Maybe said I to myself 'tis how he thinks the bed is only worked for sleep. I decided to wake him up. I shook him and pinched him high and low but you'd get better response from the pillow. I gave him a dag of a darning needle in the rump like my grandmother used to give the ass long ago and she driving him to the creamery but nothing from him saving a sigh. I dagged again and all he did was turn over in the bed. I dagged a third time till I met bone but I declare to God you'd get better results from dagging a statue. So here I am on my lonesome again. 'Twas an almighty fool that said lightning never strikes twice in the same place. What am I going to do at all. For sure you'll have to give my money back this time.

Mortified entirely,
Mrs Fionnuala Carrolane.

Hunter Hall,
Ballyninty.

Dear O'Connor,

All's well that ends well. My first skirmish with your nominee from Dead Man's Lane, namely the widow Magee, has just ended. I won't say I'm entranced but I'm bally well game to go into battle again if you can arrange a meeting. Like all women she will probably give you an outrageous account of what happened. Let us say I behaved like a man is supposed to behave and that I didn't let the side down. I am available at all times for a second brush.

Yours cordially,
Claude Glynne-Hunter.

Dead Man's Lane,
Ballylittle.

Dear Mr O'Connor

If I was to give down in full what happened in the snug at Morgan Shaughnessy's I would scandalise you surely or leave you with the eyes popping out of your head. My hayro landed with a big paper bag of toffees as you know. He ordered a drink and we fell to eating the toffees and supping

52

our whiskies. The toffees were a good quality I will say that. There is some good points to him he being sweetly spoken and well shaved and a nice smell from him likewise his shoes well shone and his trousers ironed with an edgy crease on them. All things allowed he would pass muster on first appearances. We were halfway through the bag of toffees and well into the third whiskey when he says out of the blue would you care to try another sort of a toffee. I'm sure I don't know what you mean my good man says I. Then like one of them circus quick-change artists he had the trousers whipped off while you'd be saying Jack Robinson. Sweet adorable Jesus man-alive says I is the sense after deserting you. Then I gave a look and I could see that the handle stood out straight from the belly by him and that he was dangerous. I rose and ran to the other side of the snug table. He rose too and came after me. Around and around the table we went and he chasing me. I couldn't call out in case the customers in the bar would think I was after inveigling him. All I could do was run and pray. I managed to stay in front of him. Steady girl, steady up there he would say softly now and again like he'd be talking to a mare and finally he stopped opposite me and he half-winded from the chasing. Leave me put it in a small little bit says he. I took to my heels while he was searching for breath. My one regret is that I left the toffees behind me. As I was going out the door he called after me. Steady the buffs he said. Steady the bally old buffs.

Could you remember what was the name of them toffees at all or how much a quarter are they? I left him anyway in the snug and he holding his halfpenny. What disgraceful behaviour opposite a lady. I never want to speak to him again not to mind seeing him. I don't know what came over him at all for you may be sure he got no encouragement from me. He's a quare buck to be sure. I hope you have something to say for yourself after landing me on my lonesome with that honourable ram from Ballyninty.

Sincerely,
Lena Magee.

My fine honourable boy,

I have you tagged at last. It took me a long time to get
your markings. Like a dream it was at the back of my head.
Wasn't it your ould mother that had the home for retired
asses and ponies and didn't she give the law to Kateen
Bruder of Ballyninty over she beating an ass with an ash-
plant and she trying to hurry home in a hailstorm from
Limerick city. Wasn't it that same oul' mother of yours that
saw the Black and Tans kick an innocent man to death on
the same day under the same sky on the same road and not
a word did she breathe. By Gor but she fed them asses and
ponies well when it would have been an act of charity to
put them down and while she was feeding them weren't the
children of her neighbours half starved in the cottages round
her demesne in Ballyninty, the same demesne as you have
now. 'Tis well you remember that my honourable man for
you would have been a big gorsoon in those woeful days.
You asked for a nice boy in your letters. You won't have
long to wait, a few years at most, and you'll have the nicest
boy of all looking after you, the oul' boy himself.

Courtesy and civility assure at all times.

Dicky Mick Dicky O'Connor.

*   *   *   *   *

About this time when his new career was at its zenith
Dicky Mick Dicky received his first registered letter. At the
start he was loth to accept it but upon being repeatedly assured that it was common practice to send sums of money
in this fashion he decided to sign for it. When the postman
took his leave, after refusing the offer of a mug of tea from
Kate, Dicky held the letter up to the light in an effort to
render its contents visible to the naked eye. He could dis-
cern nothing. Next he shook it but no sound came from in-

side. From under the bed in their room Kate took a noggin of Lourdes water which an itinerant clergyman had given her some years before. She thoroughly sprinkled the letter before he husband decided to open it.

Inside was a single sheet of foolscap filled with clear characters written in red ink. At the top of the letter in outsize capitals was written the terse message:'A matter of life or death'.Underneath this alarming introduction the following appeared.

Ballyoodle,
Co Clare.

Dear Mr O'Connor,

This is an emergency. If you have regard for human life you will act at once. I am to be married next Saturday fortnight to a small farmer in the next townland. My fortune is given over to his mother and all I have to do is walk in and take charge. All would be fine but for my brother Mikey who will be left alone when I go. He is fifty-five years of age with a nice place as I can verify. The brother is that he is going to set fire to himself the day before the marriage unless someone gets a woman for him. He has gallons of lamp-oil and petrol hidden in every corner of the farm and the Civic Guards say there is nothing they can do unless alone I put him out of the way by swearing him into a mental home. Sure if I do that he'll never get a woman for nobody will want him when he gets out. You are the only man in the world that can save his life. If you turn your back on him you will be guilty of murder so let you be landed here with a woman for him before Friday week or you'll have the blood of an innocent man on your hands.

Fair dues to him he's anything but choosy and any sort of an old damsel in fair working order will suit him nicely. Fail him and he'll be going to his funeral instead of his wedding. Your wages will be waiting here for you when you arrive with the woman. What he fancies is a lady that would be middling fat but firm and having a good bosom. He don't care whether she be grey, red or black nor whether bollav or chatty. You may take from all this that he is easy to please for isn't he thirty years on the trail without rising a scent. If you don't want to be a murderer and maybe swing for your crime you'll not renege on my brother.

Your sincere friend,
Agnes Tatty.

Guards' Barracks,
Ballyoodle,
Co Clare.

Dear Mr O'Connor,

I have given thirty years in the force. I am what you might call a common or garden black guard of country make. In the honour of God I beg and beseech you to find some sort of woman for Mikey Tatty whose sister Agnes wrote to you yesterday or the man will take his own life. I remember when he was thirty he threatened to cut his throat if his mother didn't give him the price of a motor bike. Twenty-seven stitches. He means business again this time. Do your utmost.

Sincerely,
Joe Doyle.

Spiders' Well,
Ballybarra.

Dear Miss Tatty,

At such short notice what you demand is impossible. I ask you now to postpone your wedding until such time as I can make out a longhair for your brother.

Your obt servant,
Dicky Mick Dicky O'Connor.

Dear Mr O'Connor,

It's no good me postponing my wedding. Mikey is determined. Unless he has his own woman by the time laid down you'll smell the burning over in Kerry and from that day to the day you die people will point the finger at you and they'll say there's the man that made a torch of poor Mikey Tatty the Lord be good to him. He has a hundred pounds put aside to bury himself and he has a grave taken in Ballyoodle graveyard. Other men will put the green scraws on top of him but 'twill be you that executed him.

Your sincere friend,
Agnes Tatty.

P.S. The reason he didn't marry up to now is that no one would have him not even the Hag Hanafin and she gone seventy-nine this Shrove and a whisker around her mouth like furze round a gap and the bare pinch of hair on her poll like the plume on a heron. You'll have a mortal hard job but you're the man that can do it if you put your mind to it. 'Tis that or put the black cap on your head and send him off to his doom.

Your sincere friend,
A. T.

Spiders' Well,
Ballybarra.

Dear Jack,

No one knows what I have gone through lately and I likely to be branded a black murderer without so much as drawing a stroke. There was this uncommonly ugly block of a man in Clare what promised to set fire to himself with lamp oil unless a woman was made out for him. I was badly caught for time only having the bare fortnight at my disposal and failing in my labours having a corpse on my hands. Hobson's Choice in dead earnest. This man's name was Mikey Tatty, clean out of his mind for a woman, as ugly a buck as ever drew on shoe leather.

Now posted in Limerick where she's in service with a doctor is a Turkish woman what weighs twenty-two stone, what drags the behind after like a fat heifer what would be going to the butcher. She came from her own country with the doctor and his wife and them what knows do maintain how she laid low her husband there with a lick of a skillet pot between the two eyes over he making out that the tapioca wasn't sweet enough for his supper. Whatever about that word came that she was anxious to marry and our man in Clare what looks like a monster in his own part of the world would be regarded as very handsome in Turkey over he having a drooping lip and yellow hide like to what they have in Turkey. Failing her there was another in Galway what had a wooden leg but was otherwise sound as a butcher's block. I threw up a penny between the two and it fell in favour of the Galway woman what was short of the leg. Off goes the pair, herself and Mikey Tatty in a hired car to view the country of Clare and to see know would they take a shine to each other. Didn't the wooden leg give under her and she facing for the cliffs of Mohar. Out she fell on her face and eyes over the cliffs and into the salt water. Devil the sign of her since, only the half of her wooden leg washed ashore in the strand of Kilkee and her name and address written down on it in marking ink in case 'twould ever be lost by her. Please forward it said to Kate Gellico, Drumdoo, Co Galway and notify a Catholic Priest in case of an accident.

The Lord have mercy on her. The Turk landed to him next and they went the opposite way to the Cliffs of Mohar, to the city of Galway to take note of the sights there and so forth and so on as the man said what went about cutting the story short.

They got drunk in Galway and 'twas there in Cummerton's public house after the consumption of seventeen half ones of potstill whiskey that Mikey Tatty pronounced his love for the Turk. They went to the altar on the very day he threatened to burn himself. His sister was the bridesmaid and her husband-to-be the best man. The bride was given away by a black man what was working in the merry-go-rounds in Galway and we put it out about him that he was her father and that he was after coming all the way from the latter end of Turkey for the wedding and that he was very high up there with a fine farm of land what was black with olives and grapes.

It would be nice a thing to say now wouldn't it that they lived happy ever after and that there was young Tattys all over the place but the opposite was to be the case. The wedding was held in Lisdoonvarna and there was lashings of drink, fiddlers from Feakle and concertina players from Kilrush. The Turkish lady threw the head sideways after she lowering the best part of a bottle of whiskey and she broke out into song. 'Twas long and high and lonesome like what you'd hear at a high mass and I declare to God there was several ullagoning like foster pups before 'twas over. It took five men for to lift her into the car and she taking off on the honeymoon to the Tatty home in Ballyoodle.

Now for the painful item. Mikey Tatty died the day he threatened but it wasn't fire that done away with him. He died accidental when the Turk turned over in her sleep, the whole twenty-two stone of her, and smothered him. God be good to him but he had little luck with the ladies. Still they say to die by fire is the worst way of all to go so that you might say he was lucky enough not to go that way. 'Tis an ill wind as the man said.

The trouble with me since he died is that I can't sleep. I done my best for him. I rose to the occasion when the sister asked me and I spread two fine bundles of daffodils on his grave what I swept out of a garden in front of a house and we coming to his funeral in the hired car. I handed over a mass card to the Turk and there's no night since we don't mention him in the Rosary. What man could do more.

Still and for all my conscience troubles me. Between them all they put me in a right pucker. If I didn't find him a woman he was faced with death and when I did fine him one he died anyway. He was doomed I suppose from the start. Mad for women all his life only to be snuffed out by one in the finish. 'Tis a cruel world to be sure. Love to Marge.

Your loving brother,
Dick.

Drombeag,
Mullachmore.

Dear Mr O'Connor,

I have a favourite to beseech you. I would like a good firm woman in the regions of thirty to forty. I have my own place a bare mile from the village of Mullachmore. It's there they have a new cinema and a parochial hall and all sorts of amusements. I work steady with a big farmer that breeds hunters and racehorses. I am age forty-two. I used to be a jockey in the flat but I have to own up I never won a race. My height is five feet feck-all and my weight is seven stone but I'm as fit as a fiddler. Would you know of anyone suitable. My cottage is in good repair and I have no shortage of anything. You wouldn't notice me in a crowd and you mightn't feel my weight but I'm a good man to do a day's work and the woman that would marry me would not want for much. There's my story long enough. If you want anymore let me know and I'll answer any question you might ask.

Yours fatefully,
Roger Speck.

Coolkera,
Coomasahara.

Dear Tricky Dicky,

No reply as yet in spite of my letters. I'm here at home this dark night after leaving Carrolane the smith to his horseshoes and his anvil. You may be sure he knocked more sparks out of one shoe on that anvil than he ever knocked out of me. I'm going to write to the bishop about you. Ordinary law isn't half good enough for you and a bishop don't charge nothing. You'll be quick to fork out my money then. There's a round and a half of it coming to me now not to mention the interest on the first lot. I want no more to do with you only hand over my hard earned money or you'll pay dear.

Fionnuala Crust.

P.S. I heard today from a tinker that Carrolane is after getting a stroke.

F. C.

Spiders' Well,
Ballybarra.

Dear Mr Speck,

Got yours today. Don't despair. Every bush will nest its own bird sooner or later. You say you wouldn't be noticed in a crowd. I pays no heed to that. There's no crowds in marriage beds only pairs. I have a woman in the back of my head for you but I'll disclose no name till I know more about the lie of the land. Being a jockey I'm sure you'll appreciate that a broken mare is better than an unbroken one. No bother to an unbroken filly to unsaddle you whereas your sound mare that's been around the course a good few times won't never dump you and you coming into the regulation if you follow. She'll get across it somehow whereas the filly might shy. I'll say no more for now Mr Speck as

61

my missus is thrown down with a heavy dose of the flu and I'm faced with an almighty amount of work.

Courtesy and civility assured at all times.

Dicky Mick Dicky O'Connor.

Hunter Hall,
Ballyninty.

Dear O'Connor,

You're very hard on me. My late mother was, as you say, kinder to asses and ponies than she was to human beings. However, you must remember that the cottiers around the demesne were a shiftless lot, lying, evasive, dirty and thieving. Small wonder that she found asses more rewarding than people. It is very easy to condemn people like me but you should remember before you commence castigation that I am as God made me. I am not run of the mill alas. I have many parallels in nature. You might say I am one of the exceptions who proves the rule that only opposing sexes should complement each other. If this is so I have my rights and I also believe that there is room under the sun for men of my inclination. God would not have placed us here if the case were otherwise. Anyway why should I have to justify myself in a world which is full of misfits without my kind. If the truth were told every man is a misfit of one kind or another and that is basically why no two men are exactly alike in outlook. Take care then O'Connor for it could well be that you and your righteous contemporaries are far more flawed than I. You judge me by your standards yet I dare not judge you by mine. Is something not rotten then in the State of Denmark and all the other states that are conditioned against that which they cannot or will not comprehend. A fair hearing old boy, an open mind. In short, a modicum of tolerance for the other fellow.

In spite of your letter I am still in the market for a wife. Do you think you could induce our friend from Dead Man's

Lane to agree to a second encounter. I promise to be on my best behaviour. I am trying hard to be what is often hopefully but erroneously labelled an ordinary man. This may help account for my seemingly extraordinary behaviour in the snug of Morgan Shaughnessy's highly respectable public house in Ballylittle. Do what you can and I shall not be unmindful of your efforts.

Do you know the name of the fair-haired boy with freckles and the buck teeth who stands regularly at the back of Ballybarra Parish Hall during the Sunday night dances. I would like to correspond with him. I haven't seen him about for some time and I am wondering if all is well with him. The last time we met there was a shortage of women (isn't there always). I asked him if he'd care for a dance but he declined with a shy smile and said that he felt too tired. I saw him no more after that.

I will be anxiously awaiting word from you, at your convenience of course.

Yours cordially,
Glynne-Hunter.

The Shamrock Inn,
Shillelagh Avenue,
Philadelphia.

Dear Dicky,

Sorry to hear of Kate's illness. You just wait. She'll be up and about any day now. Marge and me is jimdandy and nowheres, but nowheres seems as attractive as Spiders' Well country just now. We gotta freak storm here that nearly blew my goddam cobs off. You don't get no weather like this over there. This burg ain't gonna be the same for weeks. Our dear ole buddy Robert Emmet O'Bannion has been asking about you and wants to know what headway you're making on his account. I need some sorta progress report bad. It would be a crying shame if all that dough went to

those bums in the Tax Department. I had a sidekick
who used to be a private dick take a peek into O'Bannion's
background and it seems the guy's legit. Now Dicky I want
you should get a colleen for this guy and get one fast. The
Dick uncovered quite a lot about O'Bannion's parents. His
old man took a powder when the kid was only a year old.
His old lady was no angel neither. She foisted him over on
her mother and took to high-class hustling, then to middle-
class hustling and finally to low-class hustling. All this time
she visited the kid regularly and brought him expensive gifts.
The kid had no idea his old lady was a hustler. Just about
the time when she had one wrinkle too many she turned
Jennie. Maybe you ain't never heard tell of a Judas Jennie.
You know me Dickie. I was always a sucker for a good
story and I never been mean with no man nor dame but one
thing is sure. You won't never catch me going bail for no
Judas Jennie. How they operate is this. You get a fresh,
pretty young dame from some hick town in the mid-west.
She gets herself a job in the city. A lotta guys get fresh with
her but this gal don't want none o that mush. She wants
maybe a nice-looking guy with a job and then a decent
apartment and a few kids, no more than that. Come to
think of it that's what most dames want. Now some middle-
aged guy comes into the picture. Maybe the guy's a crook.
Maybe he's a businessman. Maybe he's a professional man
but sure as shooting there's two things he ain't. He ain't
broke and he ain't no gentleman. He sets his sights on this
country chick and boy does he hanker after her. Like I say
she ain't no cheap broad and she turns him down when he
tries to date her. So he goes and gets hisself the services of a
Judas Jennie, usually some hustler that seen better days.
No assin about now. He comes to the point. He wants the
country kid and he wants her bad. He's prepared to cough
up plenty provided the Jennie comes across with the goods.
Here's what happens. The old broad makes friends with the
kid which ain't too difficult when you figure the city's full
of strangers mosta them wolves. The kid begins to trust the
Jennie when she gets to know her better. Then the Jennie

gets to work. First a little drink. Next time maybe two. It ain't no harm she says. Help you relax. Sleep better. Everybody does it so what the hell. Then the little gal is introduced to night life. You got the glitter and you got the music and you got the champagne and it's all such good fun. Then the interested party is introduced casually, quite by accident. Then Jennie points out he's not such a bad ole guy. He spends plenty and he knows the best night spots. Then one night the kid gets drunk and she and the Jennie go to the guy's apartment or maybe some posh hotel. After that its all one-way sailing and soon, very soon the kid's a good-time girl. Gals like this don't never stay the distance. At thirty she's an old woman, worn out and unwanted. So you see Dick how it comes I don't cotton to this particular kinda doll they call a Judas Jennie. Ain't no job I can think of so Goddam despicable and I figure they ain't no God gonna forgive a dame does what a Jennie does. You ask me forgive a guy who maybe kills my wife I guess I'd just have to do it but a Judas Jennie never, not if she was depending on it to stay alive. Robert Emmet O'Bannion never knew how his old lady ended up. He was told by his granny that she went down with the Titanic and he believes it cos it's what he wants to believe. He's a decent ole asshole. They ain't nobody can take that away from him. He keeps buzzin me about this Irish colleen every time he comes in to the Shamrock and I don't have nothing to say to him so git on your bike Dicky and do sumpin fast. Enclosed find a get-well card from me and Marge for Kate and a few dollars to get her a bottle of brandy or some sorta tonic wine to bust that flu. Take care man.

Your loving brother,
Jack.

Coolkera,
Coomasahara.

Dear Sir,

I'm going to the bishop this very day. You got your
chance and you didn't take it. You'll be scandalised soon in
the sight of the people. Since Carrolane died I didn't sleep a
wink. He made no battle the poor man. What was he but a
big soft heap. Still there was a nice turn-out for his funeral.
I put no wreath over this one. He cost me enough as it was.
I'm going to put in for the widow's pension and resign myself to a life of celebrity and modesty but not before I put
the bishop on your tail you ingrate you that was the father
of all my misfortune.

A double widow,
Fionnuala Crust.

Drombeag,
Mullachmore.

Dear Mr O'Connor,

I'm the jockey that wrote to you for the favourite which
was to know would you be able to locate a nice firm woman for me in the regions of thirty to forty. In the last letter I forgot to tell you I have five hundred pounds in the
post office. I'm not terrible choosy so long as she's fairly
firm. I have a new tarpaulin in the bedroom and if the
weather improves I'm going to plant a sit down toilet beyond the back door so she won't have far to travel if she get
caught short. I'm surprised you never found anyone for me
and then again I'm not. I'm so miserable in size and frail in
appearance that people often mistakes me for a corpse when
I'd be lying down anywhere. Please don't renege on me, I
was told you once said that every man on the face of this
earth is entitled to a wife except them that volunteers for
the round collar.

Yours faithfully,
Roger Speck.

Dear Dicky,

She's gone sex mad. I can't keep her contented. I swear to God 'tis not in the power of one man to satisfy her since I started dosing her. Fine if I could stay in bed all day but I does have to be tending to the cows at cockcrow. The quare thing is that she don't need no dosing now. I'm like a lath from contending with her. There was one time I thought I'd never get enough of it but now I'd sooner an egg. Let me know soon if there is any way to control her.

Your devoted friend,
Thady Thade Biddy Mackessy.

Guards' Barracks,
Tullylore,
Co Cork.

Dear Mr O'Connor,

Yesterday I went through the effects of the late Cornelius J. McCarthy of Menafreghane, Tullylore. Among them was a letter from you from which I gather that you were endeavouring to find a wife for him. Mr McCarthy died in his bed a week ago tonight. It would seem that the bedclothes took fire from a cigarette which he had been holding when he fell asleep. We found his charred body a few days afterwards when his nearest neighbour raised the alarm. No smoke had come from his chimney in forty-eight hours and the neighbour went to investigate. The light of heaven to him he was a decent fellow for all his afflictions. A wife was all he wanted out of this life.

On the night of his death he had been drinking in the village of Tullylore. He hired a car to take him home. That was the last time anybody saw him alive. I hope he has better luck where he is now. No man deserves it more.

Sincerely,
Oliver Mowrey (Segt).

P.S. I'm fifty-two. I never married. My father and mother died young and my salary went to the upkeep of my younger brothers and sisters. They're all married now but here am I in my barracks with only a black cat for company.

O. M.

*   *   *   *   *

Following a strongly-worded letter from Fionnuala Crust of Coomasahara to the bishop of the diocese, the parish priest of Ballybarra, Father Andrew Dree, was summoned to the palace where he was handed the letter in question and told by his Lordship to digest its contents.

'In case', said the bishop, 'my presence imposes any constraint upon your digestion I will leave you to yourself for ten minutes after which time I will return when I will be most eager to hear your views.'

So saying the bishop withdrew and Father Andrew devoted his full attention to the letter.

'My dear Lord Bishop', it ran, ' 'Tis sorry I am to be driven to writing to you but I must reveal my tale to someone. There is a matchmaker operating in the north of the County by the name of Dicky Mick Dicky O'Connor, that pawned over two dead husbands on me and he knowing the creatures to be on their last legs. Twice I paid him the first time twenty pounds and the second time ten pounds. 'Tis an awful note in a Christian country that an honest woman can't marry legally in the Church of God without fear of ending up a widow before you'd know a man well enough to go calling him by his first name. He should be read from the altar the fifty-two Sundays of the year and faced with the bell, book and candle and at the end of that time transported to the farthest corner of Australia. If he gave me my money back itself 'twould give me some satisfaction. No indeed only going about his wicked business and splicing other poor devils that's wanting or demented or some way worse entirely. 'Tis a shame the Church don't act against this monster and they content to give out wholesale agin ordinary poor sinners that knows no better. If there isn't satisfaction I'll write to Rome to the Holy Father complaining the whole lot of ye from top to bottom. Devil the world will oul' Dree the parish priest of Ballybarra let go and he coining out of the marriages. A pity he don't ask how they're made or do he care as long as he scores for tying the knot.

A badly-wronged martyr,
Fionnuala Crust.'

At the conclusion of the letter Father Dree thrust his right hand into his trousers pocket in search of matches with which he might consign the defamatory epistle to flames which was his wont with all letters of a spurious nature. He realised suddenly that the letter was addressed to the bishop and stayed his hand in the nick of time. With barely suppressed anger he slammed the offending pages on the gleaming mahogany table where stood the bishop's pipe-rack and writing paraphernalia. He paced the study in a rage, realising he must restore himself to a rational state before the bishop's return. As in all crises he blamed his curate Father Burk. It was Burk who had several times dissuaded him from attacking the loathsome matchmaker from the pulpit by pointing out the large number of marriages which had been arranged in the parish since O'Connor had begun operations. He realised now he had been misled by his curate. But, he told himself, if a curate is responsible for directing his parish priest into an impasse should not the curate be made to shoulder the blame. It was the apparent logic of this deduction that impelled Father Dree to address the bishop with the following opening remark:

'My curate', said he, 'must take all the blame for this.'

'Your curate?' said the bishop.

'Yes my curate', Father Dree affirmed.

'But, said the bishop, 'I was under the impression that it was the parish priest and not the curate who ran the parish.'

'Granted', Father Andrew answered most amiably, 'but one is forced to depend on the advice of his curate in certain matters.

'In certain matters yes', said the bishop. 'In serious matters no.'

'I was often on the point of paying this fellow O'Connor a visit but my curate always defended him and I must confess I heeded my curate. To whom else am I to go for information. It was often on the tip of my tongue to denounce this matchmaker from the pulpit but again on the advice of my curate I relented. Now I see that I was gravely mistaken to place so much credence in the recommendations of my assistant. I did so in good faith and in the belief that respect for his opinions would mature him in good time for the day when he would have a parish of his own.'

To this the bishop listened without comment. From his face it was obvious that he was not impressed. There followed a most arduous and probing succession of questions at the end of which he placed his hand on Father Dree's shoulder.

'My dear Andrew', said he, 'a curate is but a curate. It is the parish priest who must shoulder the blame when things go wrong. Go now and never forget. I will trust you to deal with this matchmaker in your own way. I am not familiar with your part of the diocese and being a townsman the idea of matchmaking is anathema to me. In certain cases there may be some merit attached to it but the obvious pitfalls must far outweigh what little good might come from it.'

The interview ended on this note. On his arrival home Dree was greeted in the dining-room of the presbytery by Father Burk who was in the middle of a supper which consisted of two hard-boiled eggs and a plentiful supply of toast.

'Do you ever think of anything but your belly?' the parish priest shouted slamming the door behind him and at the same time calling to his housekeeper that he would be dining in his study. The curate was perplexed but not for the first time. After a moment or two of thought he resumed eating and halfway through the second egg he had forgotten altogether the castigating remark of his superior.

Bright and early the following morning, immediately after breakfast, Father Andrew summoned his curate to his study.

'We're going this morning', said Father Andrew, 'to the abode of Dicky Mick Dicky O'Connor. I am going to impress upon him the error of his ways and ask him to abandon this odious practice of matchmaking.'

'Odious', said the curate.

'Odious', said Father Andrew, angered at the pretended perplexity of his subordinate.

'You'll be exceeding your authority', said the curate.

'You're exceeding yours', said Father Dree.

'But the man is doing the world of good', Father Burk insisted. 'He's giving so much hope and the opportunity of love to so many.'

'And you're giving me a pain in the head,' Dree retaliated. 'Now when we arrive I want you to hold your tongue. I want no comment of any kind from you or you'll find yourself facing your bishop. Understood?'

'Understood.' This in a mutinous undertone from the curate. When the pair arrived at Spiders' Well Dicky Mick Dicky was drying the breakfast ware with a faded cloth.

'How're the men', he said, 'and pray tell me what I can be doing for you this handsome day?'

'I won't mince words with you O'Connor', Father Andrew started. 'I have just come from his Lordship the Bishop and I may say that he is most displeased with you. I wouldn't be at all surprised if you found yourself faced with excommunication unless, of course, you mend your ways.'

A look of horror and incredulity appeared on Father Burk's face. He turned abruptly and walked out of the house.

'What are you saying man?' Dicky Mick Dicky asked of Dree.

'I'm saying his lordship recently received a letter from a woman by the name of Crust from Coomasahara who quite rightly denounced you for the villain you are.'

71

'Lower your voice while you're under my roof', Dicky Mick Dicky cautioned.

'I will say what must be said', Father Andrew shouted. 'I came here to denounce you and denounce you I will and neither will I leave here till you recant and give over the evil practice of matchmaking.'

'Listen to me', said Dicky Mick Dicky, 'and listen good Father. My wife is ailing ever since she was struck down by the flu. For her sake I must ask you to lower your voice or else leave the house.'

'Don't you dare threaten me you heretic', Father Andrew shouted. 'How dare you join people in wedlock without authority from God or man.'

'It's you who does the joining Father and I never heard of you refusing money from them you joined. I never heard of you joining any couple without money neither.'

'How dare you talk to your priest like that. What does an ignorant clod like you know about these people you have the gall to match together.'

'I know more than you that marries them. I have known many of them all their lives and the others I know from confabbing and conversing with them. I know my people but you know nothing about them only what means they have in order to put a price on the ceremony.'

At this Father Andrew's face turned white with fury. His whole body trembled as he fought for control.

'You, you, you...', he shouted with upraised hands as he sought to find a fitting form of denunciation. But nothing would come. In a rage he strode from the house announcing at the door that he would inveigh against Dicky Mick Dicky the following Sunday from the altar. Unmoving Dicky heard the hum of the car engine on the roadway. Then silence. It was then he noticed his wife's hand on his arm. She stood beside him in her bare feet, ghastly pale, dressed only in her nightdress.

'Excommunication', she whispered. 'Is that what he said?'

'Don't take any notice of him', Dicky told her. 'Come on back to your warm bed and I'll bring you a nice mug of tea.'

In the bed she clutched her beads and twined them about her blue-white fingers. Dicky noted the lacklustre look in her eyes, her ghastly pallor, in particular the awesome whiteness of her scalp under the greying hair. Then for the first time he knew she was dying.

'Rest yourself now', he said, 'and I'll get you the tea.'

On Sunday Father Andrew denounced the practice of matchmaking from the pulpit and advised his parishioners to have no truck with a certain matchmaker since all such men were in league with the devil. His words served only to strengthen stands already well-established. Those who did not hold a brief for matchmaking grew firmer in their resolve to denounce it at every hand's turn while those who held with it decided to ignore the pleas of their parish priest. On the following Tuesday Kate O'Connor died in her sleep. Earlier the curate administered the last rites while she still retained her senses. The likes of the funeral was never seen in Ballybarra. Men who had not come out of doors for years presented themselves at the graveside to sympathise with Dicky Mick Dicky. Others came out of curiosity. Most came because the matchmaker was a legendary figure and his wife was a respected woman. All were agreed that she made a poor battle in the finish. Some maintained that red-haired people were not renowned for their resistance to illness and in her hey-day wasn't every tress on Kate O'Connor's head like a tongue of flame. When the grave was thatched with the fresh green sods which had been put aside at the beginning Dicky Mick Dicky put on his cap and without a word to anyone went home to the empty house at Spiders' Well. For several weeks he was not seen by his neighbours but there was smoke at all times rising from his chimney so that there was no fear for his welfare. If there were no smoke it could well mean that he had taken the same road as Kate. Men were known to die of emptiness before this. Dicky Mick Dicky, however, had too much regard for the life that God had given him. After two months he threw off his sorrow and faced up to the living world around him. Inside him unknown to most was a void that could never be

73

filled. No words could define the grief that lingered on but the world had to be met and life had to go on. We find him now writing to his brother Jack of Philadelphia.

* * * * *

Spiders' Well,
Ballybarra.

Dear Jack,

The black times are back again. I was never so low in my-self in all my days. She was the light of my life and the pulse of my heart. My heart breaks for her. Sometimes when I open a drawer I see a rib of her hair or a cake of fancy soap or a broach or a hairpin. At every hands turn there is some-thing to remind me of her. What am I to do at all in God's name with every day blacker than the next and the endless nights like the inside of a tomb. You have no way Jack of knowing the meaning of grief until it lifts the latch on your own door. I remember Kate and me was coming home one summer's evening from the meadow when the sky was blackened and the rain came down. We took shade under an old sycamore in the corner of the haggard. Drops of water trickled through the leaves and fell on the grass with whispers you could hardly hear. It was a slanted rain from the southwest and it didn't stay long. Soon the sun came out and lit up the water beads like diamonds on every blade of the green grass. The next thing was the birds started to sing in the heart of the sycamore over our heads and from every bush and bramble came one gay song on top of an-other. Kate took my hand and this is what she said:

'Isn't it grand for me and you Dicky', says she. 'Isn't it surely grand for you and me.'

Oh Holy Christ how am I going to endure it at all. She'll never call me again for my supper nor bring the tay to the meadows in the summer. I had great times entirely with her. I could come and go as I please the seven days of the week

74

and if I was ever in a pucker she was the woman to sort it out. God knows the value of her. 'Twas He took her. To make my cross heavier the priest read me from the altar not long before she let go of life and a nate little man what was crippled and what was a client of mine was burnt in his bed after he taking a few scoops of porter on a Sunday night. Of all the men what ever sought my services he was the one I was most anxious to supply with a companion. 'Twas hard luck on the poor fellow because I had a woman almost engaged for him and she like himself with a wasted leg but a lovely girl whatever. Another month or two and I'd have the two of them tied. This is all I have to say for the moment. I takes a few drinks every night so's I'll harvest a few winks of sleep.

Good luck and success to the Council of Trent
What put fast upon mate by not upon drink.

'Tis a deal we have something in these woeful days. Write soon and give me the news.

Your dear brother,
Richard.

P.S. I might have news of an Irish colleen for your friend. Wait for the days to grow longer and for people to turn their backs to the hearth and take the air again.

Richard.

Coolkera,
Coomasahara.

Dear Sir,
I was sorry to hear that your wife was taken from you for as bad as you are that's a misfortune I'd wish on no one. I'm here again in my own corner at the heel of the hunt as lone and lonesome as a ewe lost on the mountain. There is two things I still have after all my suas-sios and them is my two fortunes. One is my five hundred pounds and the other

is what God gave me. I do ask myself and I thrown down in front of the fire am I to be left with them forever or will I write once more to that thundering rogue that resides in Spiders' Well. Two times he harnessed me to cawbogues after landing out good money. What is your charge for a third attempt? If 'tis half price for widows surely 'tis quarter price for them that's double widows. What I'm saying is I'd be obliged to you if you was to be on the look-out once more for a suitable husband for me. Third time lucky as the saying goes. I'll be anxious to hear from you.

Fionnuala Crust (Miss).

P.S. And I pondering my problem by the fire it entered my head that the two men of mine that's underneath the sod were big, broad and weighty but still and for all they could no more canoodle no more nor a carcase and 'twasn't for the want of incitement neither for no woman ever worked harder in that line of business. My grandmother God rest her used often say the bigger the tree the smaller the apple, the smaller the bush the bigger the berry. My grandmother was no daw and I'm thinking that them you'd think you'd be made by is often the most deceitful and them that has but the bare bones is mostly the liveliest bucks of all. So don't let size be your guide no more.

Fionnuala Crust (Miss).

Shamrock Inn,
Shillelagh Avenue.

Dear Jack,
Marge and me really feel for you and we're coming for that holiday next month. We expect to be in Ireland for Saint Patrick's Day It's some day here but what the hell. You and me was always close and I guess you need company pretty bad. We can't stay no longer than a fortnight but I guess that oughta be long enough to lift you outa the

dumps and guess what! Robert Emmet O'Bannion is gonna tag along with us, not just for kicks but in the hope you'll come up with that Irish colleen. He's O.K. is Robert Emmet. All he thinks about is the colleen. I'll send a cable just so's you won't drop dead with the shock when you see us.

Your loving brother,
Jack.

P.S. I wouldn't worry none about that padre. The way he sees it you're muscling in on his territory and the way I see it is you're maybe making more hay outa the marriages than he is. Man he'd sure be cut down to size here in Philly. See you boy.

Jack.

Spiders' Well,
Ballybarra.

Dear Lena,
What would you say to a Yank. His name is Robert Emmet O'Bannion and he is most anxious for to settle with an Irish colleen. He'll be here Saint Patrick's Day with my brother Jack and Jack's wife and if I was you I'd be investing in faldals like green ribbons and green dresses with a bit of gold here and there. A good head of red hair wouldn't do you no harm neither. It might suit you better than the jet black head you have now and as I recall you looked alright when you had brown hair. He's around the seventy mark but he's not short of a shilling. You might say that he has money to burn. Let me know soon. He won't live forever.
Courtesy and civility assured at all times.

Dicky Mick Dicky O'Connor.

Dear Mr O'Connor,

I hope you haven't forgotten me. Unless the mercy of God the race of life will be run out on me without an engagement. Don't forget me.

Yours fatefully,
Roger Speck.

Spiders' Well,
Ballybarra.

Dear Fionnuala,

I have a jock for you. His name is Speck. He don't look like much. He have his own place and five hundred pounds in the post office. He's a horse breaker. By Gor says I when I read this I have a mare what will test you and that's Fionnuala Crust from Coomasahara for though the bit was in her mouth as a man said she was never rightly broke. He's only five feet tall but since he did most of his work on the flat this should be no encumbrance. There's no fear he'll drive you down through the bed because he's only seven stone. Still and for all I would say that he'll break from the starting gate like an onion fart when the white flag is raised. Remember what the oul' people say. The best of goods comes in small parcels. You had your nuff of weight and condition if ever any woman had. 'Tis time now to give a turn to the lightweights. As soon as I hear from you I'll set things in motion and as sure as there's cobs on a ram you'll be first in the frame after your next outing.

Courtesy and civility assured at all times.

Your obt Servant,
Dicky Mick Dicky O'Connor.

Dead Man's Lane,
Ballylittle.

Dear Dicky,

'Tis my fond hope that you're coming around slow but
sure after the loss of poor Kate. That the angels might sing
for her till the two of you are joined once more. I enclose a
mass card. Robert Emmet O'Bannion has the smack of a
man that might suit. Of green dresses I have plenty. I'll
wear tri-coloured ribbons for him if that's what he wants
and since 'tis Saint Patrick's Day that's nearly down on the
floor with us what's to stop me from having my bottom
painted green and my nails painted yellow. If 'tis an Irish
colleen he wants he needn't go no farther. By the way
Dicky I'm sure there's a few pounds going to you after all
the work you done on my account and if you didn't score
itself it wasn't for the want of trying. Money is a commodi-
ty I never saw enough of since the day I could first tell copper from silver so I can't offer you any at this present time.
I could give you an antique pepper caster or a napkin ring
but 'twould be a shame to spoil my fine collection especially over it having such sentimental value.

Instead of the money I could pay my account by way of
work. With your brother and his wife coming not to mention Robert Emmet the house would want a thorough
cleaning from top to bottom and the bed clothes would
want airing and there's any number of other touches that a
woman can give to a place. While you're whitewashing the
outside I could be cleaning the inside. I have my bicycle and
'tis no more nor an hour to come and less than another to
go.

Sincerely,
Lena Magee.

Dear Roger,

I must apologise for not answering your letters sooner but my excuse is that I was making enquiries on your account and in the latter end of my investigations by pure luck I came across as fine a mare as ever whinnied a stallion. She is a woman what have a fine form-sheet having as you might say been well shod for the tar road as well as the bog if you follow. Her name is Fionnuala Crust and after untackling herself from a pair of fine husbands she is getting anxious for the harness again. I can recommend this grand woman to any perspective partner as the saying goes but I may as well warn you that she'll need a tight rein if she's not to run away with you. If you could present yourself at Morgan Shaughnessy's public house in Ballylittle I will land her there at seven o'clock any Sunday or if that don't suit you there is plenty other places that might be more contagious to you. As I often told you there is an end to every road of hardship and 'tis my honest opinion that you haven't far more to go. I'll await your directions.

Courtesy and civility assured at all times.

Your obt servant,
Dicky Mick Dicky O'Connor.

Dear Thady Thade Biddy,

There's many an honest man would be glad if they had your story. There's lone men making lamentation from one end of the night to the other for the limbs of supple women and there's you discontented in the middle of plenty as the man said. I can offer no cure for what ails you beyond advising you to fire back plenty raw eggs and not to draw away from the table too soon especially if there is green cabbage going. Fish is good too and there's them oysters what does be took raw while some set great store by ground-up nutmegs. The best cure of all, of course, is to add to your present store of children. There is no cure on the face of this earth better guaranteed to knock the taspy out of a female than to place her in the family way. I hope these few hints is of use to you. The brother Jack is home from the States this past week and he was enquiring for you. Why don't yourself and herself knock over some night for a talk about oul' times. There is drink galore, all bought by the Yanks. There is the brother and his wife and there is a chap by the name of Robert Emmet O'Bannion who is sparking hard with Lena Magee. You should see her and she done up like a Crolly doll. We goes to Killarney regular. Yanks does have their dinner around the same time as we does have our supper. There is great times in it entirely just now. Jack bought a car for his stay and is giving me instructions in the use of the wheel as he says he won't carry it back with him. Won't they have nice looking at me at the creamery when I bowls in driving my car. They'll say there's great money in matchmaking. We're off again tonight. I remember the first time Robert Emmet O'Bannion asked Lena Magee out to dinner. It was shoving on for seven o'clock in the evening.

'Who in the name of God', says Lena, 'would put down spuds for you this hour of the night?'

Business is good lately. You remember the Widow Snoss, Mickeen's wife that I matched with Carrolane the blacksmith. Well I have her all but soldered to a man from Mullachmore in Cork what used to be a jockey and what has a moderate enough way of living. They're for the rails in a month. There is others as well. There is a sergeant of the Guards what was the sole support of his family but what has been free with a while to get buckled. He is stationed in Tullylore and wonders of wonders isn't his landlady a widow the bare year older than him. When I put it to him that he would be well advised in making a case to her he commissioned me to do that same. I got a warm welcome. It was how the poor fellow couldn't see the wood for the trees. If you're standing too long next to a thing you'll set little store by it. They're for the rails too very soon and no doubt he'll be arresting her one of those nights for going astray in a bed.

So 'tis well you may say that times is good. If I could only latch up Lena Magee and the Yank before the end of the fortnight you might say as how all my prayers would be answered and that I could take a stretch from my labours for awhile. I'll miss this company when they're gone back although Robert Emmet has his sights set on settling in Dead Man's Lane. So we may see more of him.

Courtesy and civility assured at all times.

Your obt servant,
Dicky Mick Dicky O'Connor.

Hunter Hall,
Ballyninty.

Dear O'Connor,

May I take it that you have severed your connection with me. Please let me know by return post if this is so as my immediate aim is to engage the services of another matchmaker.

Yours cordially,
Claude Glynne-Hunter.

The Presbytery,
Ballybarra.

Dear Dicky,

As you may have seen in the recently-published list of Diocesan appointments we are to have a new parish priest. Now that Father Dree has departed and while we are awaiting the arrival of the new man why not start going to Church again in the interim. As a personal favour I would ask you to attend Mass next Sunday.

Coolkera,
Coomasahara.

Dear Dicky,

May God increase your store and may you never see want nor sickness for 'tis you that has presented me with the liveliest man that was ever let loose in a house. The first look at him nearly put me off him and didn't I stand to the westward side of him for fear he'd be swept away by a gale of wind before he had a chance to talk to me. He was the iochtar of the litter if ever there was one. We are here now the pair of us spending our honeymoon in beautiful Coomasahara. I never knew such contentment. My grandmother was right. You might say I'm a happily married woman at long last and my one great regret is that I foolishly put quantity before quality in the past. Ah 'tis me that knows better now and 'tis me that is looking forward to a long life with my new husband. This time for sure you earned your fee. You'll hear no more out of me now.

Sincerely,
Mrs Roger Speck.

Spiders' Well,
Ballybarra.

Dear Mr Glynne-Hunter,

I never gives up on a client. Get another matchmaker if you want but I'm still prepared to work on your behalf if that's what you want. The bother with you is that you don't know what you want. As soon as you have sorted that out write to me again and I won't renege on you.

Courtesy and civility assured at all times.

Your obt servant,
Dicky Mick Dicky O'Connor.

P.S. There's a one in Pulawadra between Tralee and Listowel that might suit you. The reason I say she might suit you in particular is that I don't know what to make of her myself. Maybe you could make something out of her. She's an only daughter out of fifteen cows and a score of sheep. The father and mother is alive and they don't know what to make out of her neither. She's her own boss. That's for sure. She drives a Baby Ford. She went for a week working to Listowel when she was younger, about fifteen years ago. She came home to Pulawadra with a Yankee accent after three visits to the Astor Cinema there. She would be shoving close to forty now. There's a bit of the lady in her put there by herself, of course, and so she might suit the kind of honourable you are.

As ever,
Dicky Mick Dicky O'Connor.

Shamrock Inn,
Shillelagh Avenue,
Philadelphia.

Dear Dicky,

We just got back. Boy am I droopy. Marge is pooped after the trip but Robert Emmet takes the biscuit. He's got black circles round his eyes and it don't look like he's gonna be around for some time. That Magee dame sure spun him a funny line. Imagine asking a guy on his last legs like that to wait a year or two while she thought it over. I figure if he lasts six months he'll be lucky.

I don't think she cottoned to him all that much, not with the red eyes of his always bloodshot from shots. Come

84

to think of it he didn't smell so good neither. It sure shows money ain't everything.

We sure had a good time over there Dicky and I wanna thank you for being so all-fired nice to Marge and me and forgetting about yourself. Maybe it was best that way. I want you should go out and live and try not to think about Kate. I reckon it wouldn't do you no harm if you was to get hitched again. Kate would approve. Think about it. One thing is sure. It sure as hell beats the ass offa talking to yourself. Write soon. You hear now, real soon.

Love,
Jack.

The Presbytery,
Ballybarra.

Dear Mr O'Connor,

I haven't had the honour of meeting you yet but as your new P.P. I cannot tell you how pleased I am that you have resumed your mass-going. Father Burk speaks highly of you although I gather that you and Father Dree did not hit it off too well. I daresay this is inevitable in small parishes. There have to be differences of opinion between men of different convictions so I'll say no more about it except all's well that ends well.

Now I have a favour to ask of you. You may or may not have heard that my poor mother went to her eternal reward about six months ago. My father is still alive and lives on the farm with my batchelor brother who would like to settle down if you would be kind enough to make out a suitable woman for him. Some farmer's daughter around thirty or thirty-five would be admirable. He's a shy man. He cannot make a case for himself and this is where you can help him. I'll be most anxious to hear from you.

Sincerely,
Patrick Kimmerley, P.P. V.F.

Dear Jack,

Glad ye all got back safe. A good rest now and ye won't know yeerselves again. By God Jack but 'tis powerful lonesome since. I didn't know what lonesome was till the full loss of Kate dawned on me. I could never marry again, not after Kate. God wouldn't make two like that in the same mould. She had no equal for holding her tongue. Thank God I never asked too much of her and to tell you the truth all I would ask of a woman in excess of normal duties is that she be not given to too much talk except alone for the breaking of awkward silences. I knew a man from Mullachmore that gave up talking to his wife. He worked by signs for ten years until they became known as the Dummy Gunnells. In the end she brought him into court on a charge of cruelty. When the judge asked him his reasons for not talking to his missus his answer was that he didn't like interrupting her. 'Tis talk and talk alone what has knocked the humour and the give and take out of marriage. 'Tis a great stroke of fortune to marry a woman what has a name for talking soft and seldom. 'Tis no joke to marry a gramophone. 'Tis fine in a marriage where you have a quiet man what won't fan the flames but by the hokey where you have two with active tongues there can never be a minute's peace. I remember Kate and me went once to Ballylittle engaging a goose for the Christmas dinner. The house was to the west of the village and when we landed a small fat woman came to 'the door and got carried away at once by her own talk. We followed her into the kitchen where there was a thin man wearing a cap and he mending an ass's harness. To this day I don't know for sure who that man was, whether husband or lodger for the woman never let up spouting chatter at the top of her voice the whole time. When Kate and me thought she was tiring we would try to get a word in edgeways about the goose but the minute she saw us ready to talk off she'd go again. The man by the fire nodded his head in agreement with all she said. Fine for him said I to myself to know such contentment with a closed gob. She spoke about the geese and what she gave them to eat. She spoke about the hay and the cows and the cabbage. The likes of her cabbage was never seen.

'Of course the dung was druv on it', said she, 'double doses of it. High quality.'

Suddenly the man in the corner spoke. He took his chance nice and handy while she was drawing breath.

'Hard to beat horse's cowdung', said he, with a shake of the head.

'Hard indeed sir', said she and she went on gabbing like a blackbird you'd be after disturbing in a bush the same as if she never heard him. We drank tea and we eat bread but we left without engaging the goose. And we going out the front door she was still at it and your man in the corner nodding away like he'd be doting. The thing I'm trying to convey to you is that the pair were as happy as the day is long and that surely is what matters.

There is no meaning to the loneliness of the nights that's with us. They're hard to bear and 'tis no fun keeping a sane head on the shoulders waiting for the dawn of day to come round. Business is slacking somewhat these days. Since motor cars got common the demand is dropping but as I was saying lately to Father Kimmerley you'll always have men what cannot knot their ties or their laces proper. I made out a fine woman for a brother of his and he is most thankful. He is saying a special mass for Kate this coming Sunday. I could make no fist of that motor car you left. Everytime I sat into it it had like to run away with me. I'll stick to the ass what I was always used to. For the present I have it installed in the stable where the weather won't rust it. Tell Marge the widow Magee was asking for her.

Your fond brother,
Dicky.

Dear O'Connor,

Good news at last. That woman from Pulawadra is a lady to her fingertips if I may say so. Prospects never looked brighter and when I explained to her about my outlook so to speak she broke out into a song:

> There's a balm for every woe, sang she
> And a cure for every pain.

Since I can find no trace of my former wife high or low there is every reason to believe that the Pride of Pulawadra as the locals call her will not reject me when I pop the question. She is a poetic soul and which is more important she has the art of infusing the spirit of poetry into others. I swear I have been gliding on wings of pure poesy since I met her. I am indeed most grateful to you and have composed the following song in your honour:

> From Toomevara to Ballybarra
> From Honolulu to the Cove of Cork
> From Bulawayo to County Mayo
> From Venezuala up to New York
> From West Virginia to Abyssinia
> From South Australia to Timbuctoo
> From Ballyseedy to Tourmakeady
> There's not matchmaker could match with you.

I shall be in touch. As soon as I know my exact position there will be a more material recognition of your services.

> Cordially yours,
> Claude Glynne-Hunter.

Dear Jack,

I said I might as well write to you so that you would be
the first to know about Lena and me. Looking out the window the other evening before I sat down to my supper I
noticed the light failing in the sky and I saw the first mists
of the winter thickening on the shoulders of the hills. As far
as the eye could sweep there was nothing else to be seen
save the smoke far away from Cud Muldoon's chimney and
a straggle of pensioner crows flapping home to Parson Roberts Rookery God be good to him.

In no time at all it was dark and the strangest feeling
came over me like as if I was the only creature in the whole
wide world. My dog sat in his corner but he slept like a top
and my cat took off hunting the minute the moon shone
bright. There was no cold in the kitchen as I had the fire
bright and well-banked but for all that a shiver ran through
me that I can't explain to you. I never felt so alone. This
was something I have never felt before and I guessed that it
was the jostling between the tug of life and the tug of the
grave. I was always a man that had a dread of nothing but
the cold sweat came out through me and I made the sign of
the cross.

'Twas fear Jack, a man's fear in his lonesome state. There
is no lone man proof against that fear boy. I felt like going
to my bed and pulling the clothes over my head when I
heard a sound that was more welcome than the dews of the
morning. 'Twas the voice of Lena Magee of Ballylittle and
she cycling home after a day's visiting to Circes Muldoon.
She was singing as she cycled but 'twas a forced song because women don't care too much for the dark. There is a
bit of a rise outside the door so she dismounted and started
to walk.

'Lena', I calls out, ''tis too dark to be travelling further.'

''Tis dark alright, Dicky', said she.

''Tis', says I, 'and the forecast is not good. To make matters worse', says I, 'the mist is after falling from the hills and

in another ten minutes you won't see the back of your hand.'

She came in and sat by the fire. The cat came in behind her and he jumped on to her lap. The flames leaped in the hearth and the wind howled in the chimney.

''Tis fine for us', she said.

''Tis', said I, 'when you take all things into account.' Then that thing came between us that is beyond nature and beyond the flesh, a sorrow for each other that softens the heart and makes a bond of steel between one man and one woman.

The date is set for the Saturday before Christmas. A woman is a great thing in a house if 'twas only for wetting the tea you wanted her.

Your fond brother,
Dicky.

*   *   *

LETTERS OF A SUCCESSFUL T.D.

This bestseller takes a humourous peep at the correspondence of an Irish parliamentary deputy. Keane's eyes have fastened on the human weaknesses of a man who secured power through the ballot box, and uses it to ensure the comfort of his family and friends.

LETTERS OF AN IRISH PARISH PRIEST

There is a riot of laughter in every page and its theme is the correspondence between a country parish priest and his nephew who is studying to be a priest. Father O'Mora has been referred to by one of his parishioners as one who 'is suffering from an overdose of racial memory aggravated by religious bigotry.' John B. Keane's humour is neatly pointed, racy of the soil and never forced. This book gives a picture of a way of life which though in great part is vanishing is still familiar to many of our countrymen who still believe 'that priests could turn them into goats.' It brings out all the humour and pathos of Irish life. It is hilariously funny and will entertain and amuse everyone.

LETTERS OF A LOVE-HUNGRY FARMER

John B. Keane has introduced a new word into the English language — *chastitute*. This is the story of a chastitute, i.e. a man who has never lain down with a woman for reasons which are fully disclosed within this book. It is the tale of a lonely man who will not humble himself to achieve his heart's desire, whose need for female companionship whines and whimpers throughout. Here are the hilarious sex escapades of John Bosco McLane culminating finally in one dreadful deed.

LETTERS OF AN IRISH PUBLICAN

In this book we get a complete picture of life in Knockanee as seen through the eyes of a publican, Martin MacMeer. He relates his story to his friend Dan Stack who is a journalist. He records in a frank and factual way events like the cattle fair where the people 'came in from the hinterland with caps and ash-plants and long coats', and the cattle stood 'outside the doors of the houses in the public streets'. Through his remarkable perception we 'get a tooth' for all the different characters whom he portrays with sympathy, understanding and wit. We are overwhelmed by the charms of the place where at times 'trivial incidents assume new proportions.' These incidents are exciting, gripping, hilarious, touching and uncomfortable.

THE GENTLE ART OF MATCHMAKING
and other important things

This book offers a feast of Keane, one of Ireland's best loved playwrights. The title essay reminds us that while some marriages are proverbially made in heaven, others have been made in the back parlour of a celebrated pub in Listowel and none the worse for that! But John B. Keane has other interests besides matchmaking, and these pieces mirror many moods and attitudes. Who could ignore Keane on Potato-Cakes? Keane on skinless sausages? or Half-Doors? Is there a husband alive who will not recognise someone near and dear to him when he reads, with a mixture of affection and horror, the essay 'Female Painters'? And, more seriously, there are other pieces that reflect this writer's deep love of tradition: his nostalgic re-creation of an Irish way of life that is gone forever.

SELF PORTRAIT

John B. Keane's own story has all the humour and insight one would expect, but it has too, the feeling of an Irish countryman for his traditional way of life and his ideas for the Ireland he loves.

PLAYS

THE FIELD

THE MAN FROM CLARE

BIG MAGGIE

THE YEAR OF THE HIKER

MOLL

THE CHANGE IN MAME FADDEN

VALUES

THE CRAZY WALL

Some successful Mercier Titles

LOVE POEMS OF THE IRISH
Edited by Sean Lucy

This anthology shows those people who seem to think that
we are a loveless race, how wrong they are. It takes a wide
view of what can be called love poetry, a view which embraces
a whole landscape of feeling between men and women as men
and women, and does not confine itself to poems about being
'in love' in the more restricted meaning of that term.

THE TAILOR AND ANSTY
Eric Cross

The tailor and his wife lived in Co Cork, yet the width of the
world could barely contain his wealth of humour and fantasy.
Marriages, inquests, matchmaking — everything is here.

THE FARM BY LOUGH GUR
Mary Carbery

This is the true story of a family who lived on a farm by
Lough Gur, the Enchanted Lake, in Co Limerick. Their
home, shut away from the turmoil of politics, secure from
apprehension of unemployment and want, was a world in
itself. The master with his men, the mistress with her
maids worked in happy unity. The four little girls,
growing up in this contented atmosphere, dreamed of
saints and fairies. The story is also a picture of manners
and customs in a place so remote that religion had still
to reckon with pagan survivals, where a fairy-doctor
cured the landlord's bewitched cows, and a banshee
comforted the dying with the music of harps and flutes.

THE BOOK OF IRISH CURSES
Patrick C. Power

A remarkable blend of history, folklore and anecdote, this is above all a book about people and about cursing as an ancient and mysterious agency of their fears and hatreds.

THE PERMISSIVE SOCIETY IN IRELAND?
Emer O'Kelly

This book in which case histories are given in the form of interviews makes interesting reading and perhaps it will help us to understand why people opt out of our society, sometimes through no fault of their own.

THE SEXUAL CHRISTIAN
Urban G. Steinmetz

Controversial, hard-hitting, yet at the same time, a sensitive exploration of what it means to be sexual and christian. Urban Steinmetz gets down from what he calls his sexual rubbish dump in search of an upretending Christianity.

IRISH MARRIAGE – HOW ARE YOU!
Nuala Fennell

This book presents in a powerful, evocative and graphic way the truth about many Irish marriages. The letters come from Nuala Fennell's own files and each tells a woman's story of what it is like to be trapped in the living hell which is an Irish marriage gone wrong.

I'M NOT AFRAID TO DIE
By an Irish Housewife

I'm Not Afraid to Die is the autobiography of an ordinary suburban housewife. Over the years she has acquired a husband, reared two children and built up a happy home. On a sunny spring day her doctor, a life-long friend, confirms her fears, she is to be another victim of the modern day killer — cancer. The story starts with life and a certain amount of bravado. Born at the bottom of the stairs and reared in a cotton wool filled boot box was not a very promising beginning. Being fed exclusively on brandy and water with sugar, added a touch of luxury. Things brightened up while she was farmed out to stay with Tits Murphy in Co Cork. Tits put the whole world into perspective with one indignant wag of her huge bosoms.

TOMORROW TO BE BRAVE
J. M. Feehan

This is the story of a brave woman's fight against cancer and death. Mary Feehan was a remarkable and wonderful woman who knew she was going to die a lingering and painful death but who faced up to it with unbelievable courage and who turned her last terrible years on this earth into the greatest years of her life — years of kindness, patience, understanding and unselfishness.

Send us your name and address if you would like to receive our complete catalogue of books of Irish interest:

THE MERCIER PRESS
4 Bridge Street,
Cork, Ireland.